# NOT COUNTING
# WOMEN and CHILDREN

*Neglected Stories*
*from the Bible*

## Megan McKenna

\

ORBIS BOOKS

**Maryknoll, New York 10545**

Fifth Printing, November 1997

The Catholic Foreign Mission Society of America (Maryknoll) recruits and trains people for overseas missionary service. Through Orbis Books, Maryknoll aims to foster the international dialogue that is essential to mission. The books published, however, reflect the opinions of their authors and are not meant to represent the official position of the society.

Library of Congress Cataloging-in-Publication Data

McKenna, Megan.
    Not counting women and children : neglected stories from the
bible / Megan McKenna.
        p.   cm.
    ISBN 0-88344-946-3 (pbk.)
    1. Women in the Bible.   2. Children in the Bible.   I. Title.
BS575.M44   1994
220.8'3054 — dc20                                        93-36627
                                                            CIP

For those who have counted in my life:

My grandmother Margaret Alice Murray
My nana Alice Veronica Corrigan
My mother Marguerite Marie Freeman
My father Francis Patrick McKenna
And all the children, especially Michael John

And remembering
Tom and Sue Finnegan
who shared their mead with me

With gratitude beyond words
May their stories all come true

# CONTENTS

# INTRODUCTION

Words do not disappear. They are indelible — whether they are written on paper, inscribed in hearts, or hidden in memories. A Jewish legend says that if all the earth were quiet for just a moment, then we could all hear the voice of God echoing from Mount Sinai, speaking the words of the Ten Commandments. The sounds, form, and style would roll like waves throughout time and space, catching us today and washing over us.

The words of God never disappear. They hide among us. They have a home among us, waiting for us to recognize and hear them again. They do not disappear because they are truth and they have a life all their own, in relation to all of us and to earth. And so part of our tradition is the telling of stories, the need to say the words again and again for all generations. These words and stories have the power to pry open our minds and hearts whenever we hear them spoken aloud. Telling the story, saying the words and listening is a holy enterprise, both worship and expression of life together. This is our religion, what ties and binds our lives together.

This belief that all is story and that the story never ends is the basis for these reflections on *The Book*, the scriptures. These reflections are a continuance of the words once spoken, of the Word spoken in flesh and blood among us. For the Jewish community, this ongoing process and life of the text, written and spoken, is called midrash; technically midrash is an exposition of the underlying import of the text. There are collections of midrash — or commentary — on the text, and then commentary on the commentary. It is a tried and tested method of theologizing and reflecting on the scriptures. It assumes some knowledge or understanding of the original

1

setting and meaning, but moves on from that point, spiraling out through history and spirit to the here and now.

Midrash looks at words and phrases packed with layers of meanings and associations, with webs or networks of symbols and connections that all reveal the mystery behind the words—the reality of God speaking to us. There are many meanings in translations and interpretation but they all tell of one truth—the original meaning—God, the Great Mystery that has invited us all to dwell within this presence and share this way of life and community, as one. The words are all about us and they keep expanding to encompass more, more of meaning, more of people and life experiences and situations. They draw us beyond any boundaries of time, space, awareness, identity, or possibility—beyond and into the mystery that surrounds and envelops us. This art and science of sacred storytelling and interpretation is at the core of our religion and practice of belief as God's people.

In the Jewish tradition, a page of scripture is a map through history and through different expressions of belief. On one page we can find the original text, then questions and responses down through the centuries with commentaries on the Law (Mishna from the second century), a fifth-century commentary called Gemara with comments from Rashi (an eleventh-century exegete), and then comments by scholars in the late sixteenth and seventeenth centuries. David Wolpe, a scholar and teacher, calls it a "thicket of text" designed to be endless—to remind the reader and hearer that there is no true beginning or end to the journey of language, of study, of speaking sacred words.* The journey continues in our lives, as our experiences and interpretations are added to those of other believers and storytellers and storymakers. These words and interpretations become lifelines for us, our loved ones, and others who come after us. They are transmitted, passed on, and become confession, practice, and hope, so that others can build on our beliefs and lives of worship.

My reflections in this book are midrash, commentaries on

*David Wolpe, *In Speech and in Silence* (New York: Henry Holt and Co., 1992), pp. 116-117.

the stories of the scriptures. They are carefully selected and chosen stories that are often forgotten and the comments and reflections are by people who are often ignored and not asked for their thoughts and beliefs about their place in the stories. "Not counting women and children" — two massive groups of people in the world. Yet just being a woman or a child does not necessarily put you or me in that category of people. To belong to this forgotten group, those who reveal meaning through the community's experience, we must become like Jesus, the child of God, the Word that seeks out the lost and sides with those who have not been listened to or taken seriously as theologians.

The stories are all about Jesus, who is woman, child, and man of God — poor, midwife, mother hen, a weeping human being, and always a beloved child, vulnerable and growing in his relationship to God. The stories and images reveal to all of us how to become more human. Of course there are many other stories, not told here, but I chose these carefully as foundation stories to get us thinking like a child, a woman, a man of God, one of the poor, the not-counted, the forgotten, and so they are some of God's best loved stories. Turn the page and begin once again. . . . "Once upon a time," as the story goes.

# 1

# NOT COUNTING
# WOMEN AND CHILDREN

B efore you begin to read the text below, either to yourself or aloud, close your eyes and ask the Spirit to open your ears, your heart, and your mind so that you can hear the gospel as you have not heard it before. Then open your eyes and begin.

*When Jesus heard this, he withdrew by boat from there to a deserted place by himself. The crowds heard of it and followed him on foot from the towns. When he disembarked and saw the vast throng, his heart was moved with pity, and he cured their sick. As evening drew on, his disciples came to him with the suggestion: "This is a deserted place and it is already late. Dismiss the crowds so that they may go to the villages and buy some food for themselves." Jesus said to them: "There is no need for them to disperse. Give them something to eat yourselves." "We have nothing here," they replied, "but five loaves and a couple of fish." "Bring them here," he said. Then he ordered the crowds to sit down on the grass. He took the five loaves and two fish, looked up to heaven, blessed and broke them and gave the loaves to the disciples, who in turn gave them to the people. All those present ate their fill. The fragments remaining, when gathered up, filled twelve baskets. Those who ate were about five thousand, not counting women and children (Matthew 14:13-21).*

"Not counting women and children." People react to that phrase in different ways—some with laughter, others with anger, sadness, or disgust. Especially when read aloud, that phrase hangs suspended in the air, like bait on a hook for a fish. One person responds, "I feel excluded." Another complains, "Women and children are put in the same category." Such responses are countered, "But we are all the children of God" (theological reaction to emotion). Or, "But they all were fed and everyone was satisfied, full."

I have always loved this story. It is a amazing that in a culture where we characterize men as the dominant group—and men are still dominant in the church in many ways—that that line is even in the text. It reminds us that the scriptures are inspired by the Spirit. With a line like "five thousand, not counting women and children," perhaps the Spirit is telling us that the group which is the core of the story, the core of the experience, is the specific group that is mentioned—women and children—not the one that is left out. Furthermore, sociologists say that when you gather a crowd of men, women, and children, the ratio of women and children to men can be as high as five or six to one. So, the story is really the feeding of the thirty-five thousand!

Now if we have missed these points all these years, then what else have we missed? That's what this chapter is about, but in truth, it's what this whole book, this collection of scripture stories is about—what we've missed all these years in reading the stories, for ourselves and in community, because we have been reading them from our own perspectives of dominant cultures, races, beliefs, and assumptions. We have reacted to them without letting the Spirit loose in the text and in the context of the listeners.

But to return to the story. Here are some other questions to think about: Where did the twelve baskets come from that all the leftovers were collected in? We always remember the extra food, but what about the containers? Maybe they came from the same place that the food came from—the women and children.

Let's go back and look at some of the details in the story. There are unexpected and often unnoticed lines like that one scattered throughout the scriptures. If we go hunting and are attentive to them, they can lead us into the wild places of the Spirit where God dwells and where the truth resides, waiting for us to discover it anew. Let's go to the very beginning of our story: "When Jesus heard this, he withdrew by boat from there to a deserted place by himself." This is the immediate context for the story. It is the boundary, the setting, and the atmosphere that sets the tone for all that follows. What does Jesus hear?

He hears of the execution of John the Baptist in prison, his beheading during a banquet where Herod was entertained by Herodias's daughter Salome. In response to her dancing, Herod offers her a gift, anything she wants, and what she wants is what her mother wants—the head of John on a platter. John, the prophet who goes before the face of the Lord, the herald of the long-awaited one, is murdered at a dinner party because of a powerful woman's rage. The demise of the greatest prophet of the Hebrew scriptures is demeaning, humiliating, and part of a much larger political intrigue in which the coming of the Messiah, conversion, and the possibility of hope for the poor and the masses of people (never taken into account) are ignored. John is dead. His disciples carry away his body, and then they come to inform Jesus.

Jesus' reacts with sadness, sorrow, anger, fear; he seeks aloneness. John is his cousin, and the one who cleared the way for him—the way is now wide open. What Jesus does now is crucial. It sets in motion all future events. There must have been many things in Jesus' heart and on his mind. First and foremost he felt grief at John's murder and its utter stupidity and callousness. He felt a mixture of anger and righteous rage at the killing of the prophet, the cutting off of the voice crying in the wilderness, giving hope, and calling to repentance and conversion. Fear rises inside him; he knows that what happened to John will most likely happen to him if he picks up John's mantle of justice in the prophetic tradition and begins to assert himself as the preacher of hope and the coming of the kingdom of God. To grieve, Jesus goes off to a deserted place; he goes by himself. It is the natural, usual reaction of many people in such a situation. He needs to pray, to weep, and to remember; he must reflect and decide what he himself will do.

But the next lines tell us that he can't get away—"The crowds heard of it and followed him on foot from the towns. When he disembarked and saw the vast throng, his heart was moved with pity, and he cured their sick." Jesus was baptized by John. John had many disciples and many more followers. The people, the masses of the poor and those who hoped for the coming of the Messiah and the possibility of a new life—

religious and economic and social—are left without a leader, bereft and alone, panicking and without direction. But they know of Jesus; he has already been preaching. As soon as John is dead, the crowds turn to Jesus and will not allow him time apart. John's disciples and even Jesus' own disciples are disoriented, grieving, frightened, angry. Jesus sets out across the lake, and the need of the crowd is so desperate that the people follow him around the lake on foot and are waiting for him when he reaches the other shore.

This story is told in the context of death—needless death, death that is carried out in cold blood for political and personal reasons, death that affects thousands of people. This story situates Jesus in a political reality, a sociological reality, and a religious setting, as well as recounting his personal reaction to the death of John. What Jesus does now sets up the rest of Matthew's gospel. His reaction will affect his own disciples, the crowds and so, all of us as well. What kind of person is Jesus? He is human. And at this crisis in his life he is sorrowful, in need of solitude, wanting to get away from everyone. He needs to pray and be with his Father, grieving. But Jesus sees the vast throng, and his response is *pity*—"his heart was moved with pity, and he cured their sick." In that one phrase the kingdom begins in earnest, and Jesus' decision is made. He pities a vast throng and instead of taking time for himself and dealing with his own very deeply felt desires and needs, he turns to the crowd, knowing that when he does, he sets in motion his own eventual confrontation with the political and religious establishment and his own death. What motivates Jesus' actions, choices, and response is pity. When we grieve, we want to go off alone, to take care of ourselves. When others come after us in this situation, many of us run. But Jesus turns to them, returns with them, and spends the entire day with them. The story is about great lack, great emptiness, and great human needs in the face of suffering and death; in the face of political intrigue, manipulation, destruction; in the face of personal loss and the cry and reach of human hope in the face of life that can seem to be so terrible.

*Pity.* This word causes realms of reactions—most of them

negative. So many people don't want to be pitied. They want to be befriended, cared for, respected, attended to, ministered to, taken compassion on, but not pitied. It is a relentless word, a powerful emotion. In our culture it often connotes looking down on someone, a position of being above another person, an impersonal reaction to a problem rather than a positive response to a human being in need. But Jesus pities a vast throng of people and spends the rest of the day with them. What kind of depths does Jesus tap into in his own soul?

What is this pity that moves Jesus, even as he grieves and mourns for John the Baptist and is worried about his own future? The word *pity* in ancient languages and in today's culture has two very strong meanings, both of which can be applied to this text. The first is a gut reaction: the sight before us makes us so sick that we want to throw up. This is not what it means to live, to be human. This is not the way the world should be. This is not the way God created us to live and be with each other. It revolts us. It literally makes us sick; it moves our stomach muscles to throw up anything in our systems. Our bodies and our minds recoil and reject the situation before us. This is what Jesus feels—he looks at a vast throng and he wants to be sick. The other meaning is just as strong and evocative. The sight makes us so angry that our stomach muscles (the same ones that make us want to throw up food) begin labor contractions and bring forth something new—give birth to an alternative of hope and profoundly alter the reality before us. Jesus feels this too, and his pity can encompass a massive crowd of people: men, women and children, all directionless, afraid, lost, without hope, desperate, and in need. And Jesus spends the whole day curing the sick.

Jesus spends the day with the crowd. It's a crowd of five thousand—if you don't count the women and children. So we can picture a group of about thirty-five thousand people on foot, heading out of the towns, around the lake, trailing a man they hope can help them. They are women, children, the elderly, the poor, and all manner of others. The crowd undoubtedly includes merchants, beggars, travelers, the curious, the sick, the lame, the blind, lepers, public sinners, prostitutes, tax collectors. There are probably scribes, teachers, pharisees, lawyers, and others as well. It is humanity—a great sea of people—and they spend all day together because of Jesus' presence. He cures their sick. We sometimes think of immediate healings, miraculous events one after another. But often curing is a process that includes conversation, support, affirmation, touch, caring, time spent together listening and telling the hard truths about how we got in the situations we are in, gentleness, concern; this takes place among strangers as well as with friends and family members. Jesus cures them and a relationship begins to develop among the crowd. We know this because when Jesus tells them all to sit down on the grass, they obey him. They've been with him all day— they know him a little, and they long for his continued company. Jesus' presence in their midst levels them—from many individuals with separate needs and sickness, from many different social groupings and religious sensitivities, to just people, folk, human beings, disciples, and followers in some small measure, with him for now. They don't want to leave him. They have touched some sort of hope, some possibility of change, of graceful living in the midst of their questions, confusion, and pain.

But the disciples have other ideas. They say to Jesus as evening draws on: "This is a deserted place and it is already late. Dismiss the crowds so that they may go to the villages and buy some food for themselves." Their suggestion is blunt and seemingly insensitive. "Jesus, tell them to go home and leave us alone." The disciples have been with the crowds all day too, and they want Jesus to themselves. They, like John the Baptist's disciples, want to grieve, want to talk with Jesus, want to get their anger and fears out, want intimacy with Jesus before anything else happens. They are caught between the crowds, the larger reality of John's death, and the uncertainty of what this could mean to them as Jesus' followers.

But Jesus' reaction is clear, even blunt—probably devastating to his followers: "There is no need for them to disperse. Give them something to eat yourselves." This is the central line of the story. And as often as this story has been discussed, everyone tries to avoid this impossible line. Jesus *can't* mean what he says to the disciples! "Give them something to eat yourselves." It is not a suggestion. It is a command. It is a direction, a course of action, one that will change everything, even their thoughts about what they can do and cannot do.

We too are disciples. Jesus is also telling us to feed the crowd, telling us to do the seemingly impossible. We tend to react to his command, not by obeying, but in much the same way as the disciples do—we reject the idea with a bit of anger at the thought of being put in such an impossible position and with some frustration at not knowing what to do.

So the disciples say: "We have nothing here, but five loaves and a couple of fish." Basically, they begin by lying—we have nothing and then add on—except five loaves and a couple of fish. They have nothing—*except* enough to feed themselves. Jesus says, rather curtly, almost sounding annoyed: "Bring them here." Jesus wants their food and he wants it now. The disciples still want Jesus to send the crowds away (notice that they do not intend to try to disperse the group, they tell Jesus to do it!), and they want to eat with Jesus. They want his company—to break bread with him, alone, away from the crowds. Jesus will have nothing to do with that idea.

This portion of the story reveals to us that the disciples may have been with Jesus and the crowd all day but, unlike Jesus, it is not apparent that they have learned pity or concern for the crowd and for the people's suffering. They are still tied up in their own questions, their own emotions and needs, and they are looking for the chance to take care of themselves as soon as they can. But Jesus refuses to let them take care of their own needs first—emotionally or psychologically. He is about something else entirely. When Jesus sees the vast throng and has pity on them, he decides to act. What he does next is a model for the rest of the gospel, the rest of his life, and the life of all his disciples. We are called to the kingdom of the poor.

"Then he ordered the crowds to sit down on the grass. He took the five loaves and two fish, looked up to heaven, blessed and broke them and gave the loaves to the disciples, who in turn gave them to the people." This process, this pattern is simple—and simply unbelievable! He orders the crowd to sit down on the grass. He begins by organizing chaos, by putting them into small groups as they sit down together. Then he takes the disciple's food, small and inadequate to feed a multitude, and looks up to heaven and blesses and breaks loaves and gives them back into the hands of the disciples. He takes, blesses, breaks, and distributes them through his disciples to the people seated on the ground. The meal is served by his followers.

Of course, as someone always says, "That's liturgy! That's eucharist! That's what we do every Sunday at mass!" Yes, exactly. Feeding the crowds with what we ourselves have is exactly that—liturgy. Jesus takes whatever we have and, even if the gift is reluctant, blesses it, breaks it, and passes it around, giving it away graciously. How simple!

And "all those present ate their fill." There was enough, not only enough, but all those present ate their fill—they were satisfied, filled, content! A miracle indeed. But what was the miracle, what *is* the miracle? The story is not just about the feeding of the five thousand—not counting women and children—but it's our story too, today, here and now. The miracle is usually referred to as the "multiplication" of the loaves and the fishes. But the idea of multiplication is never alluded to in the text. Sometimes people say they have images of the disciples taking the tiny pieces of bread and tearing off pieces of the fish and giving them to people. Right in their hands the pieces get bigger and bigger and whole loaves of bread jump into people's laps and outstretched arms—shades of the movies and special effects! They laugh, but then someone soberly says: "If that didn't happen, what did?" And then the talk heats up, the theologizing begins in earnest, and the opinons and images multiply just like the bread and fish spilling out of nowhere.

What did happen? Let's go back to that phrase we began with—"not counting women and children." Men, about five thousand of them, were in the crowd. That includes the twelve disciples, who had enough food just for themselves and Jesus. They were perhaps used to Jesus heading off into the desert, or on foot to the towns, teaching and preaching, and they had learned to carry supplies for the day's outing. Most of the other men, though, probably decided to follow

Jesus that day after hearing about the death of John the Baptist; perhaps they didn't think to take food. Grief, fear, and uncertainty have a way of making us forget about the basic necessities of life. Our emotions and souls need to be taken care of before we think to eat or sleep or rest or do the normal things of everyday life. But what about the women and the children? Who are these women and children?

Even today, when women and children go anywhere, out for the morning or afternoon, shopping, on errands, to the babysitter, the women take provisions in bags—diapers, food, juice, water, change of clothes, toys, pacifier, odds and ends that they and the children consider necessities. Now women and children haven't changed much from two thousand years ago. If women and children were in the crowd, they brought water in skins or jugs, and food—bread, fish, cheese, fruit, things that could be carried easily in a bag or the pockets in robes and clothing. And just as people today always take along more than they need, they had extra. And remember, there are people carrying their sick on pallets, with bedding, slings, medicine, water, bandages, and so on. This is a motley crew, a crowd, a vast throng of unwashed poor, desperate, hungry, and sick people.

Who was counted? Who made up the five thousand? Today when crowds are counted, who's considered important, who's included? Even in the census there are thousands of people who are not counted: illegals, the poor, those who can't read, those who do not belong to a verifiable group, the homeless, those with no insurance, no social security numbers, all those who fall through the cracks of society. The text says "not counting women and children," but we can't assume that means literally women and children; it also means the sick, the elderly, the prostitutes, lepers, tax collectors, the unacceptables, the strangers, Gentiles, and outcasts within Jewish society. It means, in fact, the bulk of the crowd, the majority of the throng of people who are the followers of Jesus, desperately in need of Good News, of curing, and of being fed and given attention, love, dignity, understanding, and hope for the future.

The numbers of those not counted in our church include

all those who don't come but are baptized, those who come intermittently or when they are in desperate need, the separated and divorced, the gay and lesbian, the sick and terminally ill, the old and poor, the illiterate, the unemployed, those unable to drive, those who work when we schedule events, those who are considered not acceptable for whatever reason (wrong religion, weakness, sin, addictions, associations with others, all those we don't want to be caught with—in a crowd, at a dinner party or in church). Sometimes we don't even like to go to certain liturgies or parishes or be associated with groups of religious people—because we don't want to be categorized as one of them. Them—the uncounted, the unnoticed, the unacceptable, the unwanted, the problems, the masses of people in the world—that is what the Good News is about, that is what this story is about, that is what Jesus is about, that is what liturgy and ministry is all about.

Everybody present ate. The disciples must have been shocked, overjoyed, elated, surprised, confused, bewildered, at a loss. What happened? Perhaps with the help of the Spirit Jesus took the food of his own friends, gave it away generously (in fact, had them give it away), and the crowd saw what they were doing and brought forth their own food and supplies and shared them with those who didn't have anything or enough. And everyone was satisfied.

There was enough for everyone's need. Not only that: "The fragments remaining, when gathered up, filled twelve baskets." Ah, yes, the baskets—where did they come from? The women and children, the poor who carried them (with the food) into the deserted place in the beginning of the day.

The disciples have two jobs in this story—they distribute the food and they collect the leftovers—twelve baskets full. Twelve, symbolic of the twelve tribes of Israel, or the twelve disciples—or the whole world—more than enough to feed everyone. Miracle? What is the greater miracle—that Jesus multiplies food unnaturally or that the people see, trust, risk, hope, and share with one another? After all, this is the pattern, the ritual of liturgy. God takes our often reluctant gift—all that God's friends and disciples have, blesses it and gives it away to those who are in need. God uses the disciples as a model for behavior, of risking and trusting in a new order, a new way of being with one another and together with Jesus, who orders us to sit down together and eat with him. This story is about liturgy, about ministry, about life among the friends and disciples of Jesus in the midst of the vast throngs of people in the world, those upon whom Jesus has pity.

Our tasks are simple and concrete: we are to learn to pity one another, even in the face of violence, political events, and our personal griefs. We are to spend our days curing the sick: listening, attending, speaking words of encouragement and hope, being present, giving our time and friendship, being with others throughout the day in our own sorrows which are their sorrows as well. We are to take care that we feed others with our own resources, pooled together, even when it looks impossible, even when it's all we have and we need it for our immediate needs.

Discipleship is also about risk, about letting go and giving over what we have on behalf of others' needs, about sharing and being the first to move toward others and about giving generously and then blessing the gifts. It is about remembering to pick up the leftovers so that they don't go to waste. It means that intimacy with Jesus, the relationship of being a disciple, often means laying aside our own personal agenda and learning to pity those in worse condition than we are, and learning that intimacy with Jesus does not afford us instant access to him in our pain and suffering.

Discipleship is always lived in the shadow of evil, of persecution, of political danger, and in awareness of the economic realities of food, health care, and the human dignity of the vast throngs of people in the world who live in need. Seeing and recognition must inform all that we do, our prayer, our relations with Jesus and one another, and our reactions to what happens in the world of history and culture. Jesus will do this again and again in the gospels trying to impress upon his disciples, and upon us, the essential nature of this feeding of food and hope, of health and presence if we are to be in his company. Company means those with whom we break bread — and presence is bread too, sustenance for living together.

The quality of presence makes the amount of food, even the kind of food, almost inconsequential. Dorothy Day used to have a sign in the dining room of the Catholic Worker House in New York City: "Thank more and need less." It was changed with a marker to read: "Thank more and eat less." This is liturgy, worship, eucharist—we are to give thanks with our lives. Thank more, need less, eat less, share more, risk more, trust others, even strangers and crowds. Thanksgiving opens up a place inside of us that changes emptiness to potency and possibility, that allows us to live more simply so that others may simply live. The disciples ate—but probably from the leftovers, when everyone was finished and full. We need to eat afterward, after the others are taken care of, satisfied. Then we can sit down with Jesus and eat the leftovers.

In liturgy we often confuse the symbols of the scriptures as they are revealed in stories like this one with the gestures that we liturgically act out, often without thinking that we are contradicting the story. Eucharistic ministers are those who serve the community, feed the faithful people of Jesus, and wait on those in the crowd. But in most churches the eucharistic ministers and the priest eat first; everyone waits on them. *Then* the people get to eat. If we followed the text of the story and its symbolism, the priest and the eucharistic ministers—the public disciples—would give out the eucharist first and then eat what is left over, if there is anything left over.

Usually after a workshop on this story, there is liturgy and the priest decides to try it out, not taking the eucharist first. Usually no one even notices, and the priest is left with nothing. This is a rude awakening to what it could mean to be a disciple, a servant, to be like Jesus, who is never seen eating when he feeds the crowds or even at the Last Supper with his friends. Jesus seems to feed on more than food; he finds nourishment in presence and hope. Our liturgical ministries need to reflect the stories of scripture, so that there is a truthful consistency about our words, theology, behaviors, and lifestyles.

Jesus also takes his disciples' food and publicly has them give it away, distribute it to the crowd. Thus he teaches them a lesson in obedience, trust, and discipleship. If we follow the story, we see that to be a disciple is to have nothing that is really ours—individually or even collectively. It is all food for Jesus' use for the larger crowd, for needs and immediate hungers of others. It will probably be reluctant giving up on our part, just as it was with the disciples, but this story, like all the stories of the scriptures, serves as a corrective to the assumptions and practices we have developed without the power of the Spirit.

Liturgy and ministry is about lack—the lack of hope, the lack of bread, the lack of resources, the lack of direction, the lack of Spirit, the lack of trust, the lack of worship, the lack in the community, even among its leaders, the lack in everyone's life as a human being, the lacks in society, in politics, in religion. But this story of the feeding of the five thousand—not counting women and children—can serve to remind us that often the ones not counted are the ones with hidden wisdom, hidden powers, hidden truth, hidden hope of the future. The ones who were not counted had the food, the trust to share, the baskets for collecting the leftovers, and the need to stay all day. They had the ills and lacks that reveal the depth of the kingdom, the depth of Jesus' pity and power to cure, the food of his presence, and the delight and power of his company—making them not a vast throng, or a crowd, but a community, a eucharistic gathering. They worshiped together and saw and experienced the kingdom in their midst, in their bodies, and in their lives. The ones we don't expect much of, the ones we overlook, the ones we react poorly to, the ones we don't want to be associated with, the ones we despise, the ones we separate ourselves from (as the disciples tried to do), the ones we do not want to be with—*them*, whoever they are—are the ones who teach and evangelize us. They are the presence of God in our midst. They are the ones who hold the future in their lacks, in their hearts, and in their nearness to God. They are the poor, the privileged ones of the kingdom, the ones that God pities first and most thoroughly.

We forget that our story, our history as Christians, our testament begins with God hearing the cry of the poor in Exodus

and responding by coming down—down to save the people
who cried out to God. The cry rose from the land of Egypt
and drowned out all other cries and prayers. The cry of the
poor still rises loud, incessant, overriding all other cries and
prayers, because the cry of the poor is the mass of people, the
vast throng, the ones not counted, the ones God searches out,
the ones that God came to save. The story hasn't changed that
much; it's just gotten better and better, more clear and more
to the point. It is Good News to the poor, and the poor still
hear the stories and interpret them a bit differently from those
of us in a more dominant culture in the North, the white
countries, with their well-educated clergy and parishioners.

All the stories in this book are the gifts, the leftovers, the
fragments gathered up from many classes, workshops, mis-
sions, and retreats with the poor, the fringe folk of the church
in the North and South. They come from the uneducated; the
simple, ordinary people; the vast throng of churches in the
world that are seldom counted or considered. They are gifts
given, shared graciously, risked with me and others—students, friends, and neighbors. I share them because I must. I
have too much left over—I am too full. I have more than
enough to feed the whole world. I pass them on in gratitude,
with great reverence, with the hope that others will feed on
them, take heart from them, learn humility from them. I hope
they will lead others to read the scriptures together in small
groups and begin to put them into practice daily and together,
mixing liturgy with life, prayer with politics, economics with
curing, and ministry with service that is called forth from the
community, which demands and deserves eucharist—the
word and stories and the presence of the Lord among them.
Jesus wants everything we've got, all of life to use for more
life. Our crumbs are the leaven of the loaves. Our insensitivity
and lack of understanding are the places where the kingdom
is dying to break into us and our world. Intimacy with Jesus
demands that we start by forgetting ourselves, "denying our
very selves," that we might be able to pick up our cross to
follow him.

Strangers' needs come before ours—if we are the friends
of Jesus. Worship is as much about corporal needs as about

prayers and rituals and bread and wine offered on the altar. Our tables and refrigerators and cupboards tell us as much about our worship and relationship with God as our churches and ministries and altars. Collection baskets are connected to the vast throngs more than to our buildings and religious education programs. We are given enough in word and sacrament and community and presence to be full. Our excess, and what we do with it, reveals our worship and our reverence as much as—if not more than—our substance. Part of liturgy is creating community. That means the primary works and tasks of curing, spending time with others in need, and feeding the hungry before we deal with our intimacy needs with God on a personal or even small-group level. After, rather than before, seems to be the disciples' norm for dealing with those needs, at least according to this story of the kingdom in the midst of the crowds immediately after John's death. It is the first of many times that Jesus will put others' needs first, and the first of many times the disciples will not get the message. Who is to say that companionship is not liturgy too? All the time that Jesus spent with the crowd extended liturgy, and ritualized the taking, breaking, blessing, and giving away of the disciples' bread and fish.

Liturgy is not just words and ritual. It's taking our own hands and our own resources and feeding the person beside us in his or her basic human needs. It's very precise, very pragmatic, very ongoing in its need; this is a lifestyle of service and becoming aware of others around us, as well as becoming aware of the presence and intimacy of God and whom Jesus spends his time with, before he settles down to dinner with us. What goes into the hands of God comes back to the hands of the disciples to be given into the hands of the needy. What is given is given again and again. "A gift is not a gift until it has been given twice," is an apt Native-American saying.

The sustenance of our life is to be put into the hands and lives of others. This more than compassionate connection, this acknowledgment of being pitiful and in need together, and giving others something to eat is liturgy, is discipleship, is Jesus' way and response to violence, to grief, and to the future he brings to us. Giving ourselves more and more is what the story is about. Giving until we give out, give over, and give hope to others, who are also the gift of God's presence and source of healing to us. We are all in this together. So this is the story. Now what does this story say to us about theology? How does it question our agenda, assumptions, and behavior? To what future decisons does it exhort us?

This story starts off—as many of the really strong stories in the gospels begin—with a prophet. John the Baptist tells the truth about marriage, divorce, and sexuality to the reigning power, and he dies in an absolutely stupid chain of events for speaking the truth about these issues. First, John is jailed, because he criticizes Herod's personal behavior and marital relationship. Then, he is killed because the woman Herod unlawfully claims as his wife decides that he is "politically dangerous" because of his words about her personal life. This is what triggers the story we have just been reading. As it begins, Jesus is trying to deal with John's death. Yet, when he goes off alone, the crowds follow him. Jesus is all they have left, a thin thread that perhaps is connected to the future, a different future than the one intended by Herod and his wife and court. Rather than deal with his own personal grief, Jesus has pity on the crowd. Two things blend to-gether—prophecy and pity; these are two faces of the realities of life and death.

Pity—throwing up and birth pangs. What Jesus sees before him makes him so angry and so enraged that his entire body kicks into gear and says "NO! I am going to birth something new right here and now and I am going to show people what it is to live, even in the face of death and destruction. When Jesus has pity on the crowd he starts with the number one priority that should always operate in ministry, in economics, in politics: the curing of the sick, the attending to those in desperate need of life. We are confronted with the reality of the gospel—looking at and dealing with the basic necessities of human life, not just our life and its quality, not even the lives of those most bound to us as family and friends, but the life of all people.

The second principle of ministry, politics, and even spiri-tuality also is demonstrated in this story: Whatever the Chris-

tian community has, it has to let go of it, give away. That is
what church and community are for—giving and collecting
the leftovers. This is what ministry is—to have taken away
from us what we have been given for the use of God. We
cannot follow our own agenda, as the disciples tried to do.
Then we have the honor of picking up the leftovers, since we
believers are the first people who need to see the leftovers
and the power of God working in us. Jesus tells us that there
is more than enough to go around if we share. Sharing, economics, politics, and spirituality is what the story is talking
about and modeling for us. It tells us that the priorities of
ministry, of church, of spirituality are health care, curing and
healing, teaching and attending to the peoples' needs. This is
the meaning of the ritual of liturgy and the way we worship.
We are called to model in our small communities and church
and parishes and dioceses and universal church that this is
the alternative to the existing political, economic, and social
realities. This is where we start the kingdom.

Once again we consider the phrase "women and children,"
probably instinctively thinking *"just* women and children."
The crowds that followed Jesus included women and children
and others "not counted"—the sick, elderly, handicapped,
disabled, all the people in a society that are not making it—
and they are always the majority of the people. So when we
begin to look at priorities in church, in budgets, in ethical
decisions, in politics and programs, we must start not with
the five thousand who make sure they are counted, heard
from, and included, the ones who are clearly visible in society
or church. Rather we must look to the vast majority not
counted and not numbered and not included and not remembered. Our policies and priorities must, as the bishops' economic pastoral says, "Always be judged and tested on how
they allow that majority of people to participate in our lives
and our reality," that is, what they do for the people or what
they do not do.

Jesus is a prophet in the same tradition as John the Baptist.
He speaks to the authorities, yet he goes to the people. He
shows us the two-pronged subversiveness of the gospel and
spiritual life; we must somehow speak through structures and

laws and systems, and yet at the same time we must touch people on an individual and daily basis. It was a woman in Chiapas, Mexico, who told me that the baskets came from the women. "No woman in her right mind would head into a deserted place with an elderly person or a child or someone who was sick without taking food, drink, diaper changes, the works," she pointed out. So when the women went after Jesus, they took what they had with them. The real answers to their problems were not in the politics or the structures of the existing society, but in the people themselves, found among those who "do not count." The answers, the hope comes from the bottom up. They are the people who have struggled to live, who have barely survived, and Jesus knew that if he could take what the disciples had and share it, then the others would respond by sharing what they had. Some had brought much, some had probably brought nothing, some had only what they deemed necessary for themselves. Yet, in the sharing, the liturgy and worshiping that Jesus initiated, there was more than enough for them and for the rest of the world (symbolized by the twelve baskets of leftovers).

The scriptures are our constitution and peoples' lives are where the scriptures are put into practice. This is where we see how politics and economics should operate; then we can look to the political structures to serve peoples' needs. Jesus says, "Be cunning as snakes and innocent as doves" (Matthew 10:16). We need a little work on the first before we can really begin to work on the second. We must begin to listen and to learn how to be snakes. Snakes shed their skins. They keep changing and they hide when necessary. The Good News tells us that there is an alternative to the existing structures, and it is already in our midst. Putting it into practice in marriage, divorce, relationships, curing, food, health care, community, and sharing is the crux of the matter.

We must learn where we are. Most of us have one foot in one place and the other foot elsewhere. We must learn to be prophetic, to speak the truth to power, and to say very clearly what our priorities are: health care, food, education, community-building to help people participate in their own reality. We must be very clear about what we believe of marriage, family, sexuality, children, and life in community, knowing that we will be in opposition to other realities in the world. We must also learn pity for all of those who do not experience the reality of what we call the good life—whether it is of family or economic security or hope for the future.

More than half of all the families in the United States are not nuclear or blood-tied families. The adults are separated, divorced, single-parents, or double-parents but unmarried. The children are being raised primarily by women—poor women—who are not being compensated economically or politically, or even humanly, for being the sole provider for their families. Part of our pity must also be transferred to the legal systems, which must be forced to change their practices so that the government begins to pick up some of the slack. We need to become very critical and loud about what is done with our leftovers—money, allocations, food, education, shelter—and why. We need to start by saying that the priorities of people and this people's government are to stop wars and violence and to begin to put money into life-giving practices and programs for the ones not counted. At the same time we must be very careful that everything we do is based on pity, in the sense that Jesus showed pity, which is that strange admixture of compassion and rage, learned from the bottom up rather than the top down.

The women and the children, the poor, those not counted, are those who endure. These are the majority of a culture, a people, a nation, and of the world. And oftentimes they endure gracefully. In the Hebrew scriptures we are told that faithfulness is the criterion for holiness and worship, that faithfulness in caring for the poor, the widow, the orphan, the alien, the prisoner, the outsider, and the stranger among us is the specific criterion for how faithful and true we are in our worship. How we care for the vast throngs, for the poorest in our midst is our criterion for faithfulness as well. Many of these people—women, men, children, the poor—barely survive because of our lack of faithfulness. We are called to be faithful so that the majority of people do not have to just endure. That is the Good News. If we somehow align ourselves and our priorities and our passion for justice and our intensity of life with those who endure, then the kingdom will come in spite of our political systems and our personal reluctance to change, in spite of the lacks that exist in our communities and churches. We need to begin by anticipating peoples' needs as Jesus did, rather than being insensitive to them, as the disciples were.

The crowd that followed Jesus that day could be the same as the ragtag group of Exodus. In fact, that's probably exactly what they looked like and acted like—a crowd becoming a people on the move together, rich and poor, sick and healthy, young and old, Jewish, Gentile, outcast, sinner, and budding saints alike. They follow on foot as he crosses the water and teaches them in a deserted place and feeds them manna in the desert during the journey. This community, this people will survive by sharing, by the chain reaction of generosity, by living out of their pockets, by living with their lacks, by looking to those "not counted" for the future, for the answers even now, and for remembering the miracle that we always have enough and that there is absolute fullness in community with the presence of God among us.

As for the leaders of this strange community, everything they have, even for their own sustenance, will be taken away from them and given to the community as hope, as incentive, as initiation into the kingdom. And the people will follow and share, perhaps because they know how reluctant they were to share in the first place. The leaders learn from the community. The kingdom begins with a few sacrificing their own gifts, substance, and life, even if they do so halfheartedly, letting Jesus take it away from them. Remember, the taking is from a group of twelve, not an individual. Eucharist can't happen until someone takes a risk. That is the offering of liturgy, risking together so that all can be fed, and hope and justice and the bread of life can be given out to the world.

Originally in the early church everyone brought food to the eucharist celebration and sat down to eat together. That was one of the problems in the church at Corinth. The wealthy brought their own food and did not share with those who had less. There was no sacrifice, no sharing, no coming together, and no gathering up. Paul reminds the community:

"Don't eat and drink to your own death" (1 Cor. 11:29); that is, don't mock God by eating and taking care of your own needs first and leaving the leftovers to the poor, and then call that worship and sacrifice. Wait until the poor come and sit at table with them and eat together; then you will eat and drink to your life and death and resurrection in the Lord.

By the end of the third or fourth century Christians still brought food to church and made sure the entire community was fed. Then they celebrated eucharist. The Council of Trent stated five things are needed to celebrate eucharist: the people, the bread and wine, the word, a collection for the poor, and the priest (in that order, by the way). If one of these is missing, something is lacking in eucharist. This means that many of our liturgies aren't truthful, because often there is no collection for the poor. If we do not feed the poor the way we have been fed by God, who satisfies us with the word and eucharist and God's presence and the community, then there really is no eucharist, no body of Christ, no church. One of the ways of describing the early church was the phrase from the Didache, "See how those Christians love one another."

Once when I quoted that line from the Didache, someone interrupted me and said, "That's only one half of the statement. The rest of it is, 'There are no poor among them!'" Since then I have understood what eucharist is, what worship is, what presence is, and what ministry is—it's accompanying others, especially the poor, as one people. It is presence among the company we keep, the people we break bread with, and what we do with the leftovers. After all, who took home the twelve baskets of fragments? The presence of Jesus among his disciples was strong enough to get them to risk in their loneliness and fear and insecurity and strong enough for a crowd to obey and share once a few took the chance and showed them how. A miracle—truly.

Once when I spoke of this story with a group in San Francisco, someone remarked: "It would be a miracle if the emptiness and fear of insecurity of the northern hemisphere would open up and risk that kind of sharing!" The presence of Jesus is strong enough to bring forth the gifts and the lives of all the people who are already in the community. Everyone can be full, can have enough to live on, and there will be more left over for those outside the community. The community itself exists for the world outside. The community and the church exist as the presence of the risen Christ in the world. The church has its own needs taken care of in community, but the graciousness, the goodness of the body of Christ is more than enough to go around for everyone. If it happened then, it can happen now; it can happen among churches and nations. When we hear the words "body of Christ" and are offered bread, we are being offered the whole people as well as the person of Christ, who gives us the courage and the endurance to make the words truthful in our lives. These interpretations have been expressed over the last thirty years in many places. People have eaten this and absorbed it and in their poverty, which is more devastating than ours, usually there is enough. Even in their starving communities, there is enough for strangers and to take care of anyone who happens to be there—both offerings and sacrifices. This interpretation gives people hope. It gives them a way out, a way to live with grace.

I once talked about this passage in Europe with many theologians as well as with bishops of different denominations. They were heavily invested in other renditions and were having a terribly difficult time with this interpretation. Finally one of the bishops spoke, "This is the hardest thing for me to take and live with. I have lived all my life preaching this text, and I have to listen to someone who comes from another country, who indeed got it secondhand from someone else, tell me that the universal church is in a different place than I am." He knew, as well as everyone else gathered there, that this story, spoken in this way, has massive ramifications for theology and so for life.

Remember, all sorts of interpretations are true. And there are all kinds of levels in understanding any interpretations. But it is an adage that the one that is most true is the one that calls a person to a more radical following of Jesus, a more radical conversion of life—singularly and with others. It takes time, it takes practice, it takes change.

Jesus adds to the disciples' glimmer of understanding later

in Matthew, some time after he fed a crowd of four thousand—not counting women and children. One day the disciples forgot to bring any bread along. When Jesus said to them,

> "Be on the lookout against the yeast of the Pharisees and the Sadducees," they could think only, "This is because we have brought no bread." Jesus knew their thoughts and said, "Why do you suppose it is because you have no bread? How weak your faith is! Do you still not understand? Do you not remember the five loaves among five thousand and how many baskets-full you picked up? Or the seven loaves among four thousand and how many hampers-full you retrieved? Why is it you do not see that I was not speaking about bread at all but warning you against the yeast of the Pharisees?" They finally realized he was not issuing a warning against yeast [used for bread] but against the Pharisees' and Sadducees' teaching (Matthew 16:6-12).

Jesus usually does several things at once. He feeds the hungry, giving them the bread of justice and hope, the bread of community, a model of life, and a warning about forgetting and sliding into old traps of disbelief, lack of generosity and hope, and exclusion. He forms communion at the same time he is warning the people about teachings that mitigate against them being one body, one heart, and one mind. And he uses the images of yeast, of bread, of feeding, of crowds in his teaching. Yeast makes something rise. And so yeast is what makes the bread increase in community, and he is the yeast. Yeast needs a certain level of heat and moisture or else it won't rise; it goes flat and stale—like some peoples' teaching and practice. The bread, the yeast, the teaching has to be intimately connected to people, and their needs, not separate from them and their lives. The yeast must "raise" the bread of being with the women and children—all those not counted.

Jesus took care of the immediate needs of his community. He gave his followers lots of leftovers to share with others, to do for others what was done for them, with them. Bread given, broken, shared—this kind of bread eaten makes us hungry for justice and holiness and the honor of God and the care of the sick and the poor. It draws us into the company of those not counted. Jesus feeds us with his word, his stories, and the scriptures just as surely as he feeds us with bread, his body.

We are called to learn to chew on the word and take it into us and become the words that we attest to and proclaim and believe in. We become the bread of justice and hope for others, the leftovers, fragments meant to be taken out into the world and given away with stories of a miracle happening here and now. Amazing grace. Miracles everywhere. We daily pray, "Give us this day our daily bread," praying the words of Jesus and his friends.

There is a ritual I sometimes do with groups. I buy oranges, navel oranges that peel and easily split apart into separate pieces. I break the group into a number of smaller groups. Then I hand out a couple of oranges to each group. Some groups get one, others two or three or four, arbitrarily. The one who receives the orange peels it and separates it into segments as the groups listen to the reading of the text. Then the ritual begins. Prior to the reading the groups were told the rules of the ritual: No one feeds himself or herself—no one. As the participants listen to the text, they are to look at one another. When they hear a line that they associate, with the help of the Spirit, with someone they are with, they are to take a segment of orange and feed it to the person. There is no discussion, only the words of the text that belong to that person and the feeding of the orange. The person chews the orange and "chews" the text. This goes on for awhile. Very interesting and strange things occur. Some people get so many lines and so many pieces of orange that they are stuffed and full. Some get only one or two or three. Sometimes someone gets forgotten and gets none.

Eventually I start around the room (sometimes I read the text more than once so that the participants hear it again and again—it helps them feed folk), and I begin to collect the leftovers. Some people have lots left; some have eaten every last piece, even if their group had more than other groups. They all want to give me the garbage—the peels—but I only take the leftover pieces of orange. Then aloud I have them share and talk about what happened to them, what they learned, and what they did.

Some people refuse to feed another person or be fed. They take the orange section in their hand and feed themselves. Some learn from feeding; some are humbled by being fed. All are struck by the power of the words; the sweetness of the thought, the text, the orange; the intimacy of the group; the depth of what is shared and what passes among them, even though they do not use any words besides the text. Their eyes and hands and bodies communicate.

As they speak about what they learned, I go around and feed them more orange sections for anything they say and share with the group. There is much laughing and awkwardness. Some people keep talking, full of insights and meaning and more orange. Only on rare occasions does someone feed me; once in a rare while, someone will get up and leave his or her group and come over silently and feed me a line of scripture and an orange segment (getting the message that *everyone* should be fed). They learn that ministers and teachers and priests are supposed to live on leftovers, because they have the privilege and the honor of feeding the folk and the presence of God in the company of the people.

Once—it was the best time—a stranger who came in and was just listening to the group, picked up what was going on, went over to the garbage where I had deposited all the peels, and found one piece of orange that I missed. The person walked up boldly and fed me. I was stunned, humbled, and thoroughly delighted. That stranger taught everyone the power of the word, the action of the sharing, and the feeding of scripture and food.

People always begin to realize the practical dimensions of getting what we need, rather than what we choose or want. They experience what being full this way means, as well as the reality that somebody has to decide what to do with the leftovers (usually they are brought to the next meal and used for dessert and memories).

This ritual is simple, powerful, and to the point. Much can be garnered from it. Best of all, no one ever eats an orange the same way again; the taste of orange and the taste of the scripture is always one, and the memories are of communion, of laughter, of surprise and delight, and of the experience of eucharist.

I still get boxes and boxes of oranges and grapefruit at Christmas and throughout the year from students and friends and strangers who now connect oranges with scripture, eucharist, need, and communion — being fed and feeding others with the word of the Lord. Eucharist can be a picnic, a bag lunch, a dinner party, a feast of friends, hope for the poor, the distribution of surplus food, the noon meal at a hospitality house, a sandwich made and given from a back door as well as the breaking open of a scripture passage among a small group of believers struggling to make the stories take on their flesh and blood so that the miracle can happen again and again. Liturgy and the sacrament of eucharist are the formal expression of the daily routine and the unexpected event of Jesus' presence among "those not counted." Liturgy and sacrament express his prophecy and pity as he dwells among us.

"When Jesus heard this" is the way the story starts. When you hear this . . . is the way the story goes.

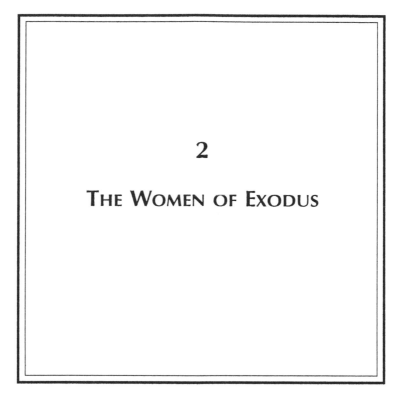

# 2

# THE WOMEN OF EXODUS

T he story of Exodus, the story of the leaving of Egypt, the plagues, of Moses, the sojourn of the people in the desert and their dream of a promised land and peace with justice for all, their memory of being saved, of being brought dryshod through the Reed Sea, and their memory of slavery kept fresh by the reality of the Law that was read to them ritually each year — all this and more is an old, familiar story. Less familiar perhaps is the Law and its demonstrable effects on the people. It was meant to be memory, memory that changed their reality and their lives, their governing and being with one another. The Code of Holiness, part of the books of Deuteronomy and Leviticus, outlined in detail how certain groups of people were to be treated — not only with justice and fairness and concern, but with active care, because these people were reminders in the present of their past plight in Egypt. They were not to treat others as they had been treated — as slaves, without dignity, without hope, without promise. The law of Jubilee, meant originally to be set into practice every seven years, was for the land and all its inhabitants, in honor of the seventh day of rest in creation. It afforded the poor and the destitute and those who had "fallen through the cracks" promise — every seven years life could begin again. All debts were cancelled, slaves were freed, prisoners were released. No land was sold in perpetuity; the land was redistributed to give everyone more of a chance. Even foreigners were offered security in the land or allowed to go home again. The land itself was rested; its crops were rotated so that the land did not grow barren and destitute.

The *anawim* — the poor of the land, including widows, orphans, strangers, aliens, prisoners — were seen, at least theologically, as the criterion for faithfulness to the covenant that God Yahweh had made with the people; the way these particular people were treated was the level and degree of faith-

fulness in the land. Later in Israel's history the prophets
would arise when the *anawim* were ignored and forgotten, or
worse, misused and mistreated or treated unjustly while the
people continued to practice their rituals of worship. Such
inconsistency offended God and the prophets, who were the
voice of God in flesh and blood and bone. These oftentimes
ornery men and women were sent to the people to confront
them with their hypocrisy and lack of true religion and worship.

The Exodus account is the source, the blood line and foundation of the Law, the ritual, and the daily life of the people,
of the covenant and the promise that continues to grow into
the hope for justice and peace in an earthly kingdom. It promises a person who will be the presence of justice and peace,
the presence of God with the people so clearly that even the
other nations will see Israel as a shining example, a light to
the world. The Exodus is, of course, about Moses and Pharaoh, about stubborn people, a collection of tribes learning in
the journeying and the desert to be a nation, a people that
belongs to God alone. But what came before? Where are
Moses' roots and source? What gave birth to the cry that Yahweh heard rising from the land of desolation and slavery?
What and who made Moses the leader of a people who also
knew the land of Egypt and Pharaoh as adopted father? Who
set the Exodus story in motion? Who was the seed of justice
and hope? Perhaps the answers will surprise you. We begin
at the beginning of the book of Exodus, where the scene, the
background for escape, for revolution and the birth of a people are hidden in another country.

> *Now Joseph and all his brothers and that whole generation
> died. But the Israelites were fruitful and prolific. They became
> so numerous and strong that the land was filled with them.*
>
> *Then a new king, who knew nothing of Joseph, came to
> power in Egypt. He said to his subjects, "Look how numerous
> and powerful the Israelite people are growing, more so than
> we ourselves! Come, let us deal shrewdly with them to stop
> their increase; otherwise, in time of war they too may join our
> enemies to fight against us, and so leave our country."*

*Accordingly, taskmasters were set over the Israelites to oppress them with forced labor. Thus they had to build for Pharaoh the supply cities of Pithom and Raamses. Yet the more they were oppressed, the more they multiplied and spread. The Egyptians, then, dreaded the Israelites and reduced them to cruel slavery, making life bitter for them with hard work, in mortar and brick and all kinds of field work—the whole cruel fate of slaves (Exodus 1:6-14).*

When this part of the story is read aloud, the silence is stunning. The description is overwhelming, exhausting, discouraging, disheartening, and almost contemporary in its description of governments and countries around the world. The state of world affairs hasn't altered significantly in hundreds of generations. The countries and the names of the dictators and the oppressed change, but there is always the reality, the stark, demeaning, and dehumanizing reality of what one people does to another—deliberately—for political and economic self-advantage. After the initial silence the discussion starts—furiously, politically, and heatedly. Suddenly the Bible is about politics, revolution, nationalism, war, slavery, and oppression. It tells of the need for hope, for promise, for escape from inhumanity. It is not just about religion, worship, and the reality of a God. The questions arise immediately: Whose side is God (our God) on and why? What does God do and want us to do in this kind of situation?

This story is not so much about individuals as about people and the way different people relate within groups in light of outside forces. It is about families, husbands and wives, men and women in oppression, and children, but not as individual families and children, but children and progeny as a political, economic, and social power or problem. And it's about history, the history of Egypt and Israel, but also all history, the history of the United States and Western Europe, Latin America, all the countries of the earth since the beginning of recorded history. There are three things to remember in dealing with the fundamental stories of the Bible, like the Exodus account, which is not only the source for all of Jewish identity, but the source of our liturgy, a passover from life and death to resurrection. The first is about the communal nature of stories. They give a people, a specific people, an identity, a corporate identity, a symbol structure, a vision and horizon as well as a past, ancestors, and source material that is unending and unfathomable in its depth. The communal interpretation and the life experience of a people, not individuals, figure more strongly than a particular interpretation or experience. This story is about an oppressed, enslaved people and what the experience did to them and still does to them (remember how Israel feels about the promised land today and consider its relationship to the Palestinian peoples). The second thing to remember is that the story is about relationships within family and about family in relation to state. Thus the story is about grandparents, parents and children, sons and daughters, siblings, aunts and uncles, in-laws, extended families, ancestors, anyone related by blood and marriage—love on physical and social levels in culture. The third thing to take into account is history, specifically war and religion and economics and the relation among these realities and their impact on families. None of us has ever lived without the reality of war going on around us, affecting us either immediately or vicariously through family and friends who fight, die, disappear, kill—or leave to avoid that choice. Religion—what ties and binds our lives together—either serves culture and dominant society or confronts and resists it, standing in solidarity with the oppressed, killed and victimized. The Exodus story is all about alliances here on earth and with whom heaven aligns itself. Now to the text.

Hundreds of years of history, generations of families and people are covered in a few lines of introduction to the book of Exodus. The previous history and the relationships that developed from the service of Joseph and his descendants are soon forgotten. The individuals are buried and lost quickly, and the group is seen as a group, not as individuals. This new king, who knows nothing of Joseph, of past alliances and connections, comes to power. Power—this is where the Exodus begins and what it's all about: political power, repressive power, oppressive power, nationalistic power, systematic power, institutional power, authority as power, and religion as power, for Pharaoh is the head of the Egyptian religion, the high priest as well as the king. And he is shrewd, calculating, and deliberate about what he's going to do. He has thought about this from a political and tactical point of view, and to keep and secure his power he will decide aright for his own future. He is concerned about the future of his kingdom and the quality of his power, and he is clear about problems that could arise to thwart it or destroy it. These must be dealt with immediately.

Someone once said in discussion of this story that she had never realized how contemporary it all was or how power recognizes and declares evil and problematic anything and anyone that threatens it. The "problem" for Pharaoh is people, overpopulation of a certain people, people other than Egyptians. The problem is race, and the response is genocide. Oh, it isn't called that specifically; it's described as "stopping their increase," and the steps taken are more subtle than murder and killing: oppress them by forced labor and slavery to build the cities, do field work, and maintain the existing economy, trade, culture, government, and society. The cruel fate of slaves is the set up for Exodus, the start of the story that has become definitive for all of Hebrew and Christian traditions even today.

*Oppressed people.* These words still reverberate in today's language and politics. These oppressed people could join our enemies, so we must do something to them now, break them now. Who are these peoples? They are what we call minorities—the masses of people who seem to multiply faster than the dominant culture does. The reaction to them is based on fear, fear by the existing power of what they will do. So the existing power makes them its enemy now. It's often called first strike—in whatever form it takes.

How do the Israelites react to oppression? The more they are oppressed, the more they increase! Their numbers frighten Pharaoh and his advisors even more, and their measures of repression mount up. Someone invariably mentions abortion here as a public policy, a way to control the population, a security measure for the rest of the existing world's guaranteed future. But in the Third World, abortion is known only as genocide, the control of their populations because there are so many more of them than the first-world countries, with their wealth, institutional power, and national security. Poverty and race and political strategies go hand-in-hand. Although individuals might make it out of poverty, groups, races, and peoples don't. They are enslaved in existing systems of economics, politics, and racism. Oppression makes the oppressor stronger, more entrenched, more secure, and wealthier. This is the historical background of the Exodus story, which now gets more specific and surprising—but in evil as well as goodness, endurance, and hope for life.

> *The king of Egypt told the Hebrew midwives, one of whom was called Shiphrah and the other Puah, "When you act as midwives for the Hebrew women and see them giving birth, if it is a boy, kill him; but if it is a girl, she may live." The midwives, however, feared God: they did not do as the king of Egypt had ordered them, but let the boys live. So the king summoned the midwives, and asked them, "Why have you acted thus, allowing the boys to live?" The midwives answered Pharaoh, "The Hebrew women are not like the Egyptian women. They are robust and give birth before the midwife arrives." Therefore God dealt well with the midwives. The people, too, increased and grew strong. And because the midwives feared God, he built up families for them. Pharaoh then commanded all his subjects, "Throw into the river every boy that is born to the Hebrews, but you may let all the girls live" (Exodus 1:15-22).*

Thus the evil expands and becomes more planned, more singular. Now genocide is to be practiced, selectively, to serve the needs of the culture of Egypt. Pharaoh begins with the existing structure of authority and power within the Hebrews—the midwives. The midwives literally have power over life and death. The Hebrews need them and honor them. There is a structure of communication and power and authority and need within the Hebrew people and the Pharaoh begins there—with the people who are links, bridges between the two cultures and races. From the way the text reads, the

Hebrew midwives performed their services not just for the Hebrew women, but for the Egyptian women as well. That kind of knowledge, skill, and power seems to lie predominantly with the Hebrews.

So power starts with children, according to this story. But male and female were used for different reasons. The boys must die, because boys grow up to fight, to be soldiers; they were the most obvious threat to the empire. Girls, however were allowed to live. Why? Girls don't fight, at least in that culture. Girls were used as slaves and for entertainment; the Egyptians intermarried with them. Girls were needed for the gene pool. We have already been told that the Egyptians were not multiplying fast enough. The culture was heavily intermarried and incestuous, especially among the ruling class. The girls were necessary and considered relatively harmless. The boys, however, were dangerous, and had to be dealt with immediately and violently. So the midwives are told to kill them as they are born; the dirty work is to be done by members of the slave nation themselves. Shades of Herod! The story has echoes that unfortunately keep ringing and repeating. There have always been societal distinctions between male and female children. Which is preferable seems to depend heavily on what is needed — fodder for war or brood mares to birth children to serve the dominant culture.

The Egyptians consider women harmless; they are useful for having more children and building up their nation. Yet we are told that the Hebrew women are robust and strong — not like the Egyptian women. And the midwives are not subservient. They collectively decide to disobey the king of Egypt, and they come up with some very interesting excuses — and he believes them! They have an enormous amount of power, even as slaves. They disobey, and Pharaoh does not punish them. They are shrewd in dealing with oppressive political power and staying alive, as well as keeping their people and their children alive. They lie a little — they say the Hebrew women deliver before they get there. Believable — after all these are slave women, field workers, hod carriers, brick layers, as well as mothers and wives. They are strong.

What is astonishing is that God is pleased with this behavior! God is delighted with the way they work together to deceive power, deal with Pharaoh, save the children, and use their power to help the people survive. So what does God do? God deals well with them; that is the women have more children, God builds up families for the midwives, and the people grow stronger. It is obvious that God is on someone's side, over against someone else.

This response to evil, to a command that is ethically and morally wrong, is blessed and acknowledged by God. In a group discussion of the Exodus story someone once brought up what Moses does when Yahweh God tells him to go to Pharaoh. He reacts fearfully and says, "I can't. I can't speak. Give me my brother Aaron to speak for me." So God does. Then God also gives him a staff, and the words to say, and the power to use the staff to threaten Pharaoh so that he will let the people go free. The women in the Exodus story do it all by themselves, and God is very pleased with them!

God is pleased with the craftiness of the midwives; God is pleased with those who keep children alive. What is it that midwives do and symbolize? They symbolize birth, deliverance, freedom, life, truth, passage. What do they do? They bring forth life, they liberate, they mediate between one world and another, they comfort. They are there in case they are needed; they are present. These midwives do all this and more. They lie to save life, and God rewards them for lying. Life is that crucial to God. They confront evil and power face to face. They keep their faith. They fear God more than they fear Pharaoh—or they don't fear Pharoah. They disobey authority. They rebel. Thus the Exodus starts. The birth canal is opened up for a people to be born and drawn through. The Exodus event and all that follows from it begins with an act of disobedience to authority that is oppressive, destructive of life, dangerous for children, and only intent on securing its continued existence. The story gets more and more specific, so that things will become clearer:

> Now a certain man of the house of Levi married a Levite woman, who conceived and bore a son. Seeing that he was a goodly child, she hid him for three months. When she could

*hide him no longer, she took a papyrus basket, daubed it with bitumen and pitch, and putting the child in it, placed it among the reeds on the river bank. His sister stationed herself at a distance to find out what would happen to him (Exodus 2: 1-4).*

Now the story shifts to a particular family. Scripture does not give the parents' names, although tradition tells us his mother's name was Jochebed, but we know what tribe they are from and that the child has a sister. This child is born into oppression, and his mother and sister will do anything and everything to keep him alive. The women take the initiative, form a strategy, and carry it out. They take the risks. The mother acts first, and then the daughter follows her lead.

This portion of the text evokes anger from both women and men. Where are the men? What are they doing? The text doesn't say—and that's deadly. The women are not submitting to Pharaoh's orders, even though they are slaves, working in the fields and cities and trying to raise families and live life. The women are mentioned, praised, remembered. What about the men? The logical and rational or reasonable conclusion has to include the thought that the men were submitting to Pharaoh's orders and killing the children as they were ordered to do. The absence of men in the description is apparent and condemning. The woman sees the child as goodly, and she hides him in the family for three months! Then the situation gets more dangerous. Perhaps even within the family circle she is pressured by relatives. She decides that she must do something else. We know that the tribe, the clan, is the Levites. This is the tribe of Israel that will become the priests of the nation.

There are numerous midrash stories about this piece of scripture, and a number of my Jewish women friends have been kind enough to share some of them with me. I have often passed them on to groups because they enhance the text and call us to deal with issues that are still very pertinent today. Midrash is commentary on the text, and there are usually more midrashim than there is text. One of them says that not only were the Hebrew men killing the male children, they were also hounding their wives to practice birth control and abortion. The midrash says that in response to this the Hebrew women banded together and refused to sleep with their husbands. (This response to infanticide is found in other cultures as well—in Greek mythology for one.) This response was the leverage the women had in the situation. The tradition goes on to say that the men were furious, and so they put away their wives, divorced them, and slept with anyone who would sleep with them, including the Egyptians. The entire family structure was disintegrating from within because of the laws and injustice from without. The tradition goes on to say that Miriam, Moses' sister, studies the Law and defends her mother Jochebed and all the other women in a court of law against her father and the other men and saves their marriages. She is considered the first woman lawyer, and she acts on behalf of the poor. She is the poor woman's advocate for justice. She, as a daughter did for her mother and the older women what they could not do for themselves.

We are told in the scripture text that she watched, that she positioned herself at a distance to see what would happen. The concept of watching, seeing, positioning has connotations of overseeing, judging, deciding aright—as God does with us. It is a decision on behalf of the oppressed within an oppressed society.

There is always a furious reaction from groups to the issue of the men either not helping the women or worse, acting in collusion with Pharaoh. This story, hardly ever told, is seldom heard or dealt with seriously. While men and women are both capable of great courage in the face of evil and great collusion, this story says that, this time the women, led by the midwives acted courageously, and consistently to protect and defend and nurture life. Thus a specific life was saved—a child who turned out to be Moses. There wasn't any remembered or noted help from the men.

After three months it's harder to hide the child. Something has to be done. The child has to be gotten rid of, but kept alive. They put him in a basket of reeds and how they made the basket is very carefully described. A young man in Honduras told me (he was reading the whole Old Testament since he had just learned how to read) that the basket that Moses is put into is made of the same stuff, bitumen and pitch, as the ark made by Noah—great symbol connection there! A mini-ark story with a woman making the boat that saves her people by saving one child.

Two woman, a mother and daughter, go to great lengths to keep this one child, their son and brother, alive. Their lives revolve around life, a specific life, and making sure he survives. This has massive ramifications for choices today. One child, any child of any woman, is worth wrapping our whole life around and keeping alive, even in the face of danger, even if it means that nothing else much gets attended to in our family.

The scripture tells stories; it does not give detailed rules about behavior. It tells of a people, of direction, of priorities and community hopes. Any group that reads a story hears the story from its own vantage point and wants the story to validate its behavior and priorities. And so men react to this story by feeling they are being judged harshly, insensitively, and not as individuals. It is interesting to note that this is the exact feeling expressed by many women in response to other stories of the scripture! But the reaction of many Western women is just as strong. They don't like the story or the interpretation, because in today's culture and individualistic society this story stands against much that many women are trying to do as men's equals, in a dominant culture. Abortion is seen as an individual choice and oftentimes the choice is decided by what effect it has on the woman's personal future and desires without the benefit of the man's input or desire or concern for the survival of any one child. Pro-choice people despise and hate this story and certainly this interpretation. It undermines their criteria for moral decision-making that allow a woman to make choices apart from any group that situates her in society and culture. Pro-life people also react. This story undermines their insistence on a woman living out this value of protecting and defending life above all else, including personal advantage, without the communal support of other women and the health-care system. Women and men must live out the value of protecting and defending life above all else.

The story has more to say—but here we see it as the backdrop for the Exodus, the story of our communal liberation, and we note that it begins very personally. These interpretations arise from people today in similar situations of oppression and domination and slavery and poverty, and these ways of hearing and seeing the story give them hope, give them strength to endure and grow stronger, and give them ways of changing their existing lives to lives of possibility, of justice and peace, in some measure. And so these interpretations must not and cannot be dismissed lightly. They put us, or our culture or country, in a light that reveals our own selfishness, loss of family cohesion, and lack of respect for life.

> *Pharaoh's daughter came down to the river to bathe, while her maids walked along the river bank. Noticing the basket among the reeds, she sent her handmaid to fetch it. On opening it, she looked, and lo, there was a baby boy, crying! She was moved with pity for him and said: "It is one of the Hebrews' children." Then his sister asked Pharaoh's daughter, "Shall I go and call one of the Hebrew women to nurse the child for you?" "Yes, do so," she answered. So the maiden went and called the child's own mother. Pharaoh's daughter said to her, "Take this child and nurse it for me, and I will repay you." The woman therefore took the child and nursed it. When the child grew, she brought him to Pharaoh's daughter, who adopted him as her son and called him Moses; for she said, "I drew him out of the water" (Exodus 2: 5-10).*

Another woman now enters the story. This time it is an Egyptian, the daughter of Pharaoh, a woman of the ruling class. The sister of the child and the mother still figure prominently; in fact, they are still intimately bound to raising the child. But we know very little about this woman from another race, another religion, another social class—except that she has pity on a Hebrew child and has the power to raise it as her own in her society. She too disobeys the law, the king, and her father. In common with the slave women: she shows pity and makes the choice to disobey. She takes life, a child, close to her and holds it there.

Many men cannot believe the story is unfolding the way it is. They cannot believe that life is that hard for any woman, any group of women. Women may react to their disbelief, angrily, spewing out statistics about rape, incest, abuse, poverty, malnutrition, and lack of health care for women and children, about the lack of child support and poor training and inferior education, about decreased possibilities for jobs and a future. They speak of the culture of poverty and what has come to be described as the feminization of poverty. They describe a climate of fear, of insecurity, of anger and rage and helplessness, of living where violence can alter a woman's life drastically and radically, without warning or recourse. Often it takes a good deal of time to get such a group to listen again to the text and what it is saying. Whenever the stories of scripture hit home they hit hard — either confirming our experiences or revealing a reality and experience that is not in our experience or that opposes our experience. Each person hearing the text takes it personally and reacts personally. The split between men and women in culture and in the church is inevitable. It is a living present reality, and perhaps stories such as these can balance and offer alternatives, ways to communicate that will open doors to unity and hope.

Pharoah's daughter takes in a Hebrew child, disobeying her own father. Why? How could she do this and get away with it? Why does she act in collusion with her father's enemies? What is her relationship with Miriam and Jochebed? Is there some sort of communal statement about life, about children, that crosses boundary lines with women? This woman acts in collusion with a mother and daughter to keep a child, a dangerous child, alive. Why? She has status, power, wealth, prestige, and place, even in the Pharaoh's own household. What doesn't she have? What does she lack? For many women, even well-placed ones, the answers are dignity, human value, worth on a personal level, relationship, love, and a future. Perhaps she cannot have children, or her child has died or been born deformed, not acceptable. She is probably one of many daughters of Pharaoh, for the ruling class

members had many wives. The women did not participate
publicly in court, in politics, or economics, though they had
power personally, depending on marriage status and closeness to the throne. For whatever reason, she joins the con-
spiracy—three women conspiring together—to hide a child's
true nature and identity over a long period of time, creating
relationships of protection and mutual aid in the face of
authority. The word *conspire* means "to breathe the same air."
That is what these women are about—saving a life, a child
who will grow up to be Moses, a liberator for one people and
the man who causes the downfall and humiliation of another
ruler of people.

This is dangerous. These women have crossed over religion, race, and economics. Together they are undermining the
government and the power of Pharaoh, the culture, and the
future. Pharaoh's daughter "drew him out of the water"—
just as a midwife does. She is a midwife too, though in another
way. She saves him just as surely as his mother and sister,
and she introduces him to a new world, another culture, language, race, religion, and life. She names him—she who has
no name in the story. She is a woman first—before she is an
Egyptian or one of the ruling class. She adopts him, so Moses
is her child, the grandson of Pharaoh! In the Jewish midrash
she is seen as the first single-parent adoptor, one who opens
the way for Moses to become the liberator, the leader of his
people. She gives him access to the culture, the system, the
life. Eventually he would use everything he had learned to
set his people free, to persuade Pharaoh to let the people go.
His education, his training, his power, his future come from
her choice, her adoption, and her binding herself to him as
his mother.

Moses is the son of an Egyptian woman *and* the son of a
Hebrew slave woman. He lives always in two worlds, two
cultures, two races, two religions, and he will be the bridge
out because the daughter of Pharaoh was his bridge in. She
accepts his own mother to nurse him and gives him back to
the family to raise until he is weaned. She is intent not only
on the child living but that he live in his own culture. She
protects him from Pharaoh and the Egyptians and from the

Hebrews who might harm him as well. Then she brings him into her own household to raise him.

In Latin America I've heard this referred to as "pushing your privilege"; acting in this way leads to salvation just as surely as being poor or oppressed. It will usually get a person in trouble with his or her own culture, economic class, and familial group, but a person can usually do it for a good while before anybody finds out.

Traditionally, the daughter of Pharaoh is known as Bithiah, and she goes with Moses and the Israelites out of Egypt into the desert. She chooses her adopted son's God and covenant as her own, rejecting Pharaoh's rule. She takes her power and uses it for and with those, who are powerless.

Five women: Midwives *Shiphrah* and *Puah*, who disobey authority that is evil and oppressive to protect life. *Jochebed*, Moses' and Miriam's mother, wife of a Levite, a Hebrew who disobeys and uses all her resources, including her daughter, to save a child, her son. She shelters a prisoner, harbors a fugitive, and hides a convicted felon from the authorities. She is willing and able to push Moses beyond her protective circle into another culture so that he might live. *Miriam*, a daughter and sister, protector, guardian, shrewd and at least as crafty as anyone in power, watchful and a servant of life; even, perhaps, willing to serve Pharaoh's daughter so that her brother can live. And *Bithiah*, a daughter, apparently unmarried or childless or both, who knows pity that goes beyond borders, laws, religious and political practice, even blood lines, who knows herself as a sister to other women, even slave women, and uses her power to protect and aid a child in growing up—a very dangerous child who will cause her to change all her allegiances and her life. All of them are midwives, and all of them say one thing very loudly in the story. To be a woman is to nurture, bring forth, protect, and defend life in every way—anyone's life, any child's life, especially any child others think to do away with and destroy. This is at the heart and core of what it means to be a human being and a woman—a midwife.

In many places, particularly among poor people, especially women, this story is used to look at how women should do

theology and what the scriptures have to say about the nature
and power of women in structures that do not allow them
access or equality or dignity. Some of their insights are startling and surprising, life-giving, death-defying, threatening to
existing structures, and annoying to both men and women
across borders and boundaries.

Poor women know that scripture calls us individually and
collectively to a radical change of life, to more life, deeper life,
truer life. They do theology based on the choices and experiences of these five women. They acknowledge that children
must be protected at all cost, and authority must be confronted so that everyone can move always toward life, more
life. These women are a source of a new approach to life, to
living with evil and surviving in danger. They are courageous.
They have nothing but each other — and God — to stand
behind them. They are ingenious, they plot and plan, they
check out ahead of time, they think imaginatively and creatively, and they cross boundaries of race, religion, economics,
and politics They make bridges where there were none before.

In this story there is no difference between personal and
political choices. The needs of the community, the protection
of life, a courageous commitment to truth and life and the
people, and natural law do not come before the law of God —
fear of God — but are the bases for moral choices, both personal and communal. These are the priorities of life, of religion, and of people. Evil must be confronted, must be resisted;
avenues must be opened up so that newness, life, birth, revolution, and liberation can be brought forth. Power must be
used for good, for life, for the future, even in oppressive situations. Coalitions, crossing boundaries, and pushing privilege on behalf of others — risking, trusting to intuition, and
treasuring life, even among strangers — these are the ways of
transforming reality, of opening up liberation. The women in
the Hebrew scriptures, if looked at closely, prefigure the Messiah. But all the stories challenge us, as believers, as community, as church, as country, as individuals, as men and women.
The scriptures are true, and so everyone, male and female, is
confronted, judged, put on the spot, called to conversion and
repentance. Often the theology that develops from reflection

on this text by poor men and women is devastating in its critique of first-world theology, no matter by whom it is done, because the issue is not seen so much as one of gender but of power and place and dominant culture.

The responses of the poor are clear, pointed, and sometimes hard to listen to. They speak of women who betray their humanness and do not protect or nurture life. Rather than acting as midwives such women vie with men in the existing power structures for more power, personal privilege, and separateness from anyone who is poor and oppressed. Some responses speak of the experience of women in the church who claim to speak for all women who want ordination, equal power in the existing structure, and changes in vocabulary and especially in the names we call God. They speak of women who say they have no power—at least not the kind they want in the dominant culture and the ways of being church—without ever criticizing the underlying basis of church practices. They speak of women with power, education, privilege, and access to the system who seem only to want more rather than looking to the masses of women who do not have the same priorities they do. They say that what is wrong with the world is wrong with us! What is wrong with the church is wrong with us! We do not examine our own lives, our own priorities, how we do things, and how we go after change, change that seems immediately to benefit us. We do not take the poor into account. We do not remember that we are women in the dominant culture.

The poor speak of men who are in collusion with the system, content with its inequalities as long as they can work it for their own advantage. Why, they ask, aren't reality, government, policies, and individuality examined from the vantage of the gospel, where everyone is found to be lacking and called to conversion? Our self-righteousness is appalling, and so is our lack of intimacy with the poor. The rest of the world, the oppressed, might see our lives within our dominant culture, both country and church, as evil. They remind anyone who listens that if the scripture doesn't bother us, we didn't hear it, and that if we don't decide to do something about what we hear, then we did not really hear it and do not

believe it. The scriptures should bother everyone, as individuals and in the groups we are aligned with. The scripture is
the word of the Lord. When and if we hear it by the power
of the Spirit, it is prophetic and judging and always unset-
tling. Scripture is always about good and evil, about giving
life and dealing death. This Exodus story is about men and
women facing an edict of death, and how these women, all
midwives, set in motion the passover, the liberation of a people. It is remembered so that others in the same situation in
history may know what to do and whose side God is on today.
Where are we? Who are we? What bridges do we make? What
coalitions do we belong to? What risks do we take? What in
our life and our daily choices protects children and life? What
groups do we belong to that put us sometimes in jeopardy so
that others can live? Do our resources, power, and relationships and our religion—how we fear God—serve those who
are vulnerable and oppressed, the masses of people, not the
advantaged or our own personal lives?

Three types of people arise in most groups that look at the
scriptures this way. The first questions, "What is this story
asking of us?" But the second, the prophet, says, "You aren't
going to like this, but . . ." And the gatherer says, "I don't like
this at all, but we have to get together and do this and stay
with it, because it's true." So the group persists until hope
surfaces and insight and the Spirit prevails and the way opens
up for them to move individually and as a community. This
breaking of the word is the source of decisions and life and
is done before breaking bread and sharing wine in community.

Jewish tradition says that God is a midwife who drew the
people through the waters of the Reed Sea and brought them
into a promised land and new life and made them a people.
And Jewish women say that God Yahweh got the idea of how
to do it from the Hebrew midwives. Often I have heard people who know nothing of the Jewish tradition put the connections together and say that God is a midwife. God watches
us and takes delight in us. What can we do to be midwives
in turn? It doesn't matter if we are male or female. Being a
midwife is about being human, and the Exodus is about being

human and living in freedom and dignity with hope and life, ever more abundant life. The story will continue, deepen, and expand but the basis is there in the beginning. It only gets more and more powerful. Yahweh, who hears the cry of the poor in bondage — of any people in bondage — always responds and leans down, comes down to bring the people forth into life. The story will be told, and it will come true. It will. It has, and it will again. Where are the midwives today?

There are still many theological issues and ideas to look at. The word *Exodus* means "going forth from." The word *pharaoh* means in Hebrew, "to exterminate," "expedient," "useful," "tyrant," and "oppressor." The word *Egypt* recalls the place of bondage. No longer are the Hebrews just people or a nation or a country, though that is still looked at, but now they are a way of being in religion, in society. Life must be put under the watchful eye of God, judged, and altered radically for communities that believe in these stories. They allow God to act in history again, to use power on the side of the midwives and the children and the ones needing to be born and brought into community as a people that belongs to God and to no other.

This particular passage is often used to teach how to do theology; it helps a group learn to set priorities within the scriptural context for use in today's society and history. It can be used to look at scriptural priorities and contrast them with those operating in a group. This is the comparison method or gospel-based critique. Another method is to examine the major characters and determine what they symbolize, and to look at what they do and how they do it. This is usually followed by listing what we can do, individually, collectively, or in small groups, and then systematically as institutions. Let us use this second method and make a few comparisons. First, what is the symbolism of each person in the story?

• Midwives: life, birth, connections, babies, service, skill, process, relationship, mediacy, tradition, knowledge, need, lack of access to usual methods, power, freedom, solidarity, shrewdness, fear of God, truth-telling, work and organization together as a subgroup.

• Miriam: sister (word sister comes from word meaning "to mend"), women in crisis, breakdown of family relations, action on behalf of others (especially those older and younger), intergenerational, boundary breaker, bridge, advocate, watchful, resourceful, creative.

• Jochebed: mother, wife, illegal actions though justified, risk-taking threatening to self, family, and state, force to be reckoned with, long-term subversive action, works together and uses all resources including daughter and position of slave, immediacy, connection to incarnation and possibility of future for people, recognition of goodness and hope and liberation, sanctuary, sees child as separate entity rather than just her child.

• Bithiah: passageway, bridge, new tradition blended with old (or alien tradition), solidarity with the poor, "push your privilege," barter (money for food, nurturing the child when she cannot), educator, teacher, shares her status, bloodline and inheritance, transition place of acceptance, adopts another as own, coalition work, life for the future.

All the above women are midwives.
Second, what do they do? Here are some answers.

1. Mediate between the king and the people.
2. Disobey orders that are unjust or the cause of death. They defy death and authority. They are systematic and organized; they work collectively, not alone.
3. Save lives (boys) as the immediate priority.
4. Work the system, know its loopholes; take matters into their own hands. They use their wits; they tell the truth when they can and lie when necessary to save life.
5. Make friends and recognize soul kin wherever they might be.
6. Recognize evil for what it is and how it operates.
7. Continue to serve and then make themselves indispensable.
8. Compensate one another for work and services.

9. Carry information back and forth among groups, structures above and below.

What does God do in response? God extends their power, enhances it, helps them, blesses them, is pleased with them, rewards them publicly in the community, helps them in their work and livelihood. God is pleased with nonviolent resistance and creativity among those who fear only God, or fear God more than any power on earth. God is pleased when they stall for time and don't let others know what they are doing; when they learn new perspectives on life, cross cultures, and take risks for life, even if their stand is unpopular. Ignoring evil orders is good. So is knowing one's priorities and where one stands: life, children, the future, protection of mothers and anyone in need because of systemic violent authority, such as the poor and those enslaved. The unorthodox or noninstitutional knowledge and wisdom of the midwives (all information connected to birthing, sustaining life, and helping to grow) is honored in God's community. Compassion is influenced by race, culture, and poverty as well as gender. The primary endangered species is humanity. Carefully thinking and acting communally is to be encouraged.

What does the Exodus story tell us about priorities? For one thing, we must take *action on behalf of life.* Population control is most often just simple and plain genocide connected with slavery and race. Abortion is not an option. But the style of our opposition is crucial. It must include nonviolence, care, compassion, service; it must cross boundaries and social structures, and push privilege rather than indulge in blaming or public exposure. Second, we must look anew at *economics,* seeing the value in barter, money for milk, presence when needed, shared responsibilities for raising children, push privilege, share inheritance, and promote education. Each does what he or she can for the child and the family. Everyone in the family helps, older ones taking responsibility as they can. We devote a great deal of time, effort, and risk to children, because they are the future and the hope in the present reality.

Third, what does all this imply for *ministry*? Pastoral practice sometimes seems to contradict the prophetic call to truth. The bridge between the two—the practical and the ideal—is the community and support groups of other families and single people that cross economic, social, even religious and race borders.

Finally, in what ways does the Exodus story cast light on government? Law is the lowest common denominator and usually a policy of expendability. This is revealed in lack of support and care in the basic areas of medicine, time, a living wage that provides dignity and support for single-parent families. Current immigration policies and lack of appreciation for nontraditional forms of service, birthing, and medicine— for the poor especially—are also issues. Political promises are usually just words, and one-issue politics blurs the issue of dignity for persons and life for all as a priority.

What are the church's, parishes' and ministers' priorities today in light of this story?

Where are the economic subsidies, voice, support groups, theology, and spirituality that would give foundation to what this story proclaims? What is giving generously in these cases regarding children and family? What is the church's attitude toward medicine, health care, midwifery, and sanctuary for those not protected by the government or in danger because of government policy?

What are the priorities of the women's movements in society and the church in comparison to the priorities of the women in the Exodus account? What is the men's movement saying that might or might not fill in the spaces in the story? What constitutes family? Where are cross-cultural and cross-class bridges being built? How are single people brought into issues of children's birth and welfare and growth? How is nonviolence as a practice of life and virtue taught in this story, and what is its connection to the Exodus?

In the next line of the story the emphasis shifts to Moses:

*On one occasion, after Moses had grown up, when he visited his kinsmen and witnessed their forced labor, he saw an Egyptian striking a Hebrew, one of his own kinsmen. Looking about and seeing no one, he slew the Egyptian and hid him in the sand (Exodus 2:11-12).*

The story reveals two things: first—that growing up consists in witnessing pain, injustice, and slavery, and seeing it for what it is; and second, Moses acts in the tradition of his upbringing and teaching as an Egyptian, a ruler; that is, he kills. The story of Exodus as it begins with the man Moses begins in an act of violence. This is in direct opposition to what all the women of the Exodus practiced, preached, and staked their lives on.

Let us return for a moment to Miriam, Aaron's and Moses' sister. She is described later in the book of Exodus and mentioned twice in the journey through the desert.

*The prophetess Miriam, Aaron's sister, took a tambourine in her hand, while all the women went out after her with tambourines, dancing, and she led them in the refrain:*

*Sing to the Lord, for he is gloriously triumphant;*
*horse and chariot he has cast into the sea.*
*(Exodus 15:20-21)*

Miriam is a leader on the journey, along with Moses and Aaron, just as she was in the community while it was still in Egypt. Here she is the leader of song, response, and dance. She is described as a prophetess—one who watches, sees, knows, and reveals to the people what is happening to them. She has been doing so since she was young; now her gift is recognized and accepted and joined by the other women. All the Israelites sang the song, and the women chanted the refrain. The role Miriam plays in liturgy is based on the work she has done in her life. Later we see Miriam and Aaron again, though not in such a positive light, in a very controversial piece of the Exodus account. It is found in Numbers 12 and referred to as the jealousy of Aaron and Miriam.

*While they were in Hazeroth, Miriam and Aaron spoke against Moses on the pretext of the marriage he had contracted with a Cushite woman. They complained, "Is it through Moses alone that the LORD speaks? Does he not speak through us also?" And the LORD heard this. Now, Moses himself was by far the meekest man on the face of the earth. So at once the LORD said to Moses and Aaron and Miriam, "Come out, you three, to the meeting tent." And the three of them went. Then the LORD came down in the column of cloud, and standing at the entrance of the tent, called Aaron and Miriam. When both came forward, he said, "Now listen to the words of the LORD:*

> *Should there be a prophet among you,*
>    *in visions will I reveal myself to him,*
>    *in dreams will I speak to him;*
> *Not so with my servant Moses!*
> *Throughout my house he bears my trust:*
> *face to face I speak to him,*
>    *plainly and not in riddles.*
> *The presence of the LORD he beholds.*

*Why, then, did you not fear to speak against my servant Moses?"*

*So angry was the LORD against them that when he departed, and the cloud withdrew from the tent, there was Miriam, a snow-white leper! When Aaron turned and saw her a leper, "Ah, my lord!" he said to Moses, "please do not charge us with the sin that we have foolishly committed! Let her not thus be like the stillborn babe that comes forth from its mother's womb with its flesh half consumed." Then Moses cried to the LORD, "Please, not this! Pray, heal her!" But the LORD answered Moses, "Suppose her father had spit in her face, would she not hide in shame for seven days? Let her be confined outside the camp for seven days: only then may she be brought back." So Miriam was confined outside the camp for seven days, and the people did not start out again until she was brought back (Numbers 12:1-15).*

After that the people set out from Hazeroth and encamped in the desert of Paran.

This episode is upsetting to many who make Miriam a heroine without any blame or faults. But all these people are people—human, weak, and gifted. They waffle and stumble and rise up again, learning as they go along. Undermining Moses' authority with the people because of jealousy is their sin. But why is only Miriam made a leper? Many people respond that she should have known better. From the picture given of Aaron and Miriam, Miriam is the stronger of the two, the leader, and so she is singled out for her actions and words and punished by God. She is a prophetess, but she has overstepped her authority in wanting the same kind of relationship with the people (and/or God) that Moses has—which seems to be unique in the Hebrew scriptures, seeing God face-to-face. The community knows what has happened, and the whole community waits on her shame and punishment. Public power and authority is dealt with publicly, Now it is Moses who intervenes for his sister and asks God to heal her. She is healed, but the point is made—even to the comparison that she now resembles a newborn babe born deformed and half consumed (words that are often used to describe jealousy). This short piece adds another idea to the issue of power, authority, and obedience, shared and not shared in the presence of the community.

The Exodus account is set in motion forty years earlier (traditionally) with Moses' birth by courageous women making moral and ethical decisions and putting their lives on the line so that others can live. They are midwives whom God watches, and then imitates, in bringing God's people through the Reed Sea. The story is shaped by the man Moses, the baby who was saved in the reeds by ingenious women, slave and free, of two nations: Egypt and Israel. The Exodus is about God's saving power expressed in all of us, sometimes very strongly, startlingly so. The story needs to be remembered and honored, not only because of the past, but because of its message for today's world. Children worldwide need a chance to be born and to be kept alive so that they might grow up to be the liberators of the people, male and female, prophets and prophetesses, leading the community to freedom and hope of life.

# 3

## Unless You Become Like a Little Child

T his book is about women and children, but not just any woman or any child. In fact, just being a woman or a child may not put a person in this particular theological category. This chapter will look more closely at the concept of child: child as Jesus uses the word and image; child as Jesus was the child of God, his beloved father; and child as we are invited to become as brothers and sisters of Jesus, the child of God in our midst, child as born of the Spirit of God. This concept of child is both simple and humble. It is a concept that is foreign and often unacceptable to modern society. But let's begin with a story. It is from the Jewish midrash, and it explains something of how precious the children of the Jews were and tells of their relationship to the community and to God. I've also found it in children's books, and a rendition of it is in *A Child's Book of Midrash*.*

*Once upon a time, in the time that we dwelled in the desert, awaiting directions for the rest of our journey to the promised land, our leader Moses came back from the mountain, where he went often to visit God. He returned excited. He gathered all the people together and announced that God wanted to give us a gift. It was called the Torah. Moses wanted to know if we, the people, would accept the gift without knowing what it was or even knowing what we were to do with it once we got it. There was a great discussion among the people—a gift from God! Of course we'd take it. After all, it was God who brought us out of the land of slavery and made us God's own people. We were God's people now. The people spoke up and said to Moses that he could tell God they would accept the gift, even without knowing what it was or what they could do with it. Moses went back up the mountain. And the people waited.*

*Barbara D. Goldin, *A Child's Book of Midrash: 52 Jewish Stories from the Sages* (Northvale, N.J.: Aronsen & Jason, Inc., 1990).

*They waited in hope. What could this be, this Torah? They knew something of the gifts of God already — manna in the desert, water from dry springs and rocks, and freedom and hope. What would this gift be like?*

*Finally Moses returned and gathered the people together again. Moses didn't have anything with him, nothing in his hands. It was very quiet, and Moses spoke when one of the leaders asked, "Where is the gift?" "I told God what you said — that you'd take the gift, but now God would like a gift in return, a guarantee that we will cherish it and use it and keep it and live with it." The people were quiet, wondering and thinking, what in the world could they give God as a gift, a guarantee of their acceptance. Almost immediately a cry went up — "Gold! jewels! all the treasure we took with us from Egypt! We'll give God that." And so the people gathered all their jewels and treasure and Moses carried it up the mountain. The people waited and wondered if God would accept their guarantee.*

*Moses returned with the great sack still full of their jewels and treasure. Moses said, "I gave God your gifts, and while acknowledging that the gifts were valuable, God would like something more, something different as a gift. After all, we can just collect more of these things." The people were quiet and the quiet lasted longer this time. Then someone spoke up: "Moses, we do have things that are more precious to us than jewels — gifts from our parents and friends, treasured possessions that are irreplaceable, singular and unique to each of us; things we value so highly that we'd never think of selling them. We would only give them away as a gift to someone we trusted and were thankful to and loved. We could give those as gifts to God as our guarantee." The people agreed, and they all went to their homes and carefully chose the best to give to God. Once again the pile grew at Moses' feet. Moses took all the peoples' gifts and climbed back up the mountain of God. The people waited. And Moses returned again — without the promised gift! "What," someone cried out, "no Torah still?" Moses waited for quiet and spoke again: "I told God that we'd be delighted to take the gift, and I gave God our treasured possessions as gifts. But God says that while the gifts are treasures* to us, they aren't guarantees that we will take and keep God's gift all our lives. Is there something dearer still to us?" There was a long, heavy silence while the people thought and reflected. The silence stretched out and then, all of a sudden, a baby cried. It was wet and tired and hungry. At this, the woman who held the child on her shoulder cried out: "That's what we can give God—we can give him our children! They can be our guarantee that we will take God's gift and keep it and cherish it. We will give it to our children and teach them to take it to heart and keep it and live by it." The people rejoiced. This certainly was the best they could give, the guarantee that God would not refuse. So Moses went again to the mountain, empty-handed but with a full heart. While he was gone, the camp sang and hummed with activity, and the people waited expectantly.

Moses returned and in his hands were stone tables that were etched deeply with words, shining words that seemed to fly off the stone and have a life of their own. Moses stood in the midst of the people and spoke: "God was pleased with our gift of our children. He has taken them as our guarantee, and in exchange he has given us the Torah—God's words, laws, and hopes for us as a people. We are to take them and learn them by heart and teach them to our children. Now these two things are intertwined forever: the Torah and our children. Together they are our guarantees in our covenant with God and our most treasured possessions."

"And so it is, to this day, that the children of Israel are taught when very young to listen to the word of the Lord, the Torah. Whenever they hear the word, they are fed something sweet, for the word of the Lord is sweet to the taste and sweet in the life of every Jew. Every generation gives God the assurance of its acceptance and keeping of the gift by giving God their children as a guarantee that they will keep the Torah and live by it, in memory of their grandparents' first acceptance of God's gift, when they still didn't even know what it was God wanted to give them. And so it still is and will be, as long as the Torah lives and the people of God live (Midrash Rahbah Song of Songs 1:4).

There is a tight connection of children to the people, the covenant, and God in Israel that is promised to endure forever. The children of Israel are the children of God—the children of the promise and the children of the covenant. Generations of Jews have looked upon their children with faith, with delight, and with hope. They are the present and visible reminder of the Torah and the law's fulfillment in their lives. The practice of the Torah in their community and in their children's lives is part of their own relationship with God. The children belong to the people and to God as much as they belong to any one family or set of parents. Children are a communal heritage and gift. This is one of the strongest understandings of children in the Jewish community.

And yet there is another understanding that seems almost in opposition to this relationship and privileged position. In Near Eastern cultures—among Bedouin tribes and in Palestine even today—the place of the child is marked and fixed within the community. These cultures and many others see a child not as an individual with rights but as part of the community, fitting at the bottom of society. In fact, the word in Aramaic for "child" and "servant/slave" is the same. Society at the time of Jesus too was structured and developed hierarchically and in strict adherence to the community and its needs. It was a tight-knit group that knew and operated on levels, and on obedience and belonging—and children were on the bottom.

There is an example in Thomas Aquinas's *Summa* that illustrates this point, and many exegetes refer to it when teaching about Hebrew culture at the time of Jesus. Thomas asks a theoretical question: If you were in a burning house with your mother and father, wife, and children, and you could save yourself and only one other, which one would you save? Of course the question was directed to men only—but it makes the point. When I ask this question today the answer is either the spouse or one of the children. No one answers mother or father—not ever. And yet, Thomas's answer is father, then mother, then wife, then child—in that order, the order of priority of love and obedience as understood in the past and in many cultures today in the present.

It is a very modern concept in the Western world that the child — the future — is important and in a position of privilege. In the past the child was seen as belonging to the father, the family, the group, and the community — not to the future. The father, the head of the household, the spokesman for the family and the group ruled. Many times in the Acts of the Apostles and in other places in the Christian scriptures we read of a man and his whole family being baptized. In Africa and other countries today, when a man is baptized, his wives and children, his whole household, cousins, aunts, uncles, and in-laws are baptized as well. Culture dictates the group response held by the one in charge, the one responsible for the others. Obedience is usually immediate and unquestioning. Western culture is drastically different and oriented toward the individual and the future and so such choices and behavior are seen as unacceptable, intolerant, aberrant, confining, and so on. But it was the norm in ancient societies and is still the norm in many cultures. Historically, children were the property of the parents and had no rights, no life besides survival and connection to adults. The current reality of child labor that still exists among the poor, migrants, factory workers, and others in many countries today attests to that understanding and lack of awareness of the individual's rights, especially among adults who have no rights. The children of the poor are doubly endangered.

All of this background is crucial to understanding the power of Jesus' words about being a child and his use of children to describe and illustrate belonging in his kingdom and his Father's house. Children were the hope and solace and comfort of parents in their old age, but life was hard and sometimes mere endurance. The struggle to live was communal and familial, unlike the individuality of today and the small nuclear families or single-parent families of much of present Western society.

Perhaps the difference today is that children, while treated singularly in families, are communally neglected and endangered and impoverished without the benefit of belonging, even at the bottom to the community or group or extended family. The statistics are appalling. Domestic violence, abuse of children, malnutrition, homelessness, and lack of education and health care for children are high and growing by leaps and bounds yearly. The United Nations considers anyone up to the age of fifteen a child, and they are the majority of people in the human race. Half the population of Nicaragua is under fifteen—more than a million and a half children in a country of three million. Each day in the United States almost 150,000 children bring guns to school; nearly three thousand see their parents divorced; thirty-five hundred run away from home, choosing the violence of the streets over the violence in their homes; more than 100,000 are homeless; seventeen hundred are in adult jails; four to five die from abuse, a dozen from guns, and more than thirty from poverty; and nearly two thousand are abused and neglected.*

Just being born and staying alive is a problem. Twenty-six hundred children are born each day to unmarried women; eight hundred are born to those with inadequate prenatal care, and eight hundred or more are born at low birth weights. Seventy of those children will die before they are a month old. These statistics are old—five years or so—and do not include children born with HIV or those whose mothers are drug addicts. About one out of every four children in the United States grows up with one parent. One out of every five lives in poverty, and among minorities that figure is higher, much higher. Forty percent are at risk of failure in school, and about seven million adolescents are involved in "high risk behaviors"—drugs, alcohol, crime, gangs, and promiscuity. And this is not just among the poor. Figures from 1992-93 reveal that the middle class is struggling with the same realities. Family structures, moral values, health care, poverty, and the dangers of childhood are all interwoven and harder to deal with in a society that is bent on individuality. Even in the United States the cry of the children is the cry of the poor. Infant mortality puts the United States among the

---

*Most of these statistics and those that follow are from "Putting Children and Families First: A Challenge for Our Church, Nation and World," issued by the U.S. Bishops in 1992 and quoted in the *Benedictine Resource Center Newsletter*, 1992.

last twenty Western nations, and the United States has the highest divorce and teenage pregnancy rate in the world. Teen suicide has tripled in the last thirty years. Being hungry, underfed, and without health insurance is more the norm than the oddity. In 1992 the bishops of the United States announced that they would be a voice for those without one, and they singled out specific areas that needed immediate attention: poverty, joblessness, lack of access to affordable health care, child care, decent housing, and discrimination. Political areas include tax policies, child labor laws, racial discrimination, gender discrimination, education, health care, and housing.

Outside the United States the needs are even greater and the numbers more depressing because of the consequences of economic policies and military actions. The reality of childhood anywhere is shaped by vulnerability, dependence on the rest of society, the need for unconditional love, and basic survival needs. It is children who are sacrificed first in economic and military maneuvers. It is children who suffer because of the adults' decisions and actions.

Isaiah says: "Yahweh called me before I was born, and named me while I was in my mother's womb . . . Yahweh said to me, 'You are my servant, Israel. Through you I will show my glory' " (Isaiah 49:1-3). We no longer associate these words only with Isaiah or the prophets, but we have appropriated them for each of us as individuals in our relationship with God. The reality of God become human, become a child among us — helpless and in need of care, protection, and a family, and place to grow up safely — has over the centuries opened up the depth of what it means to be a child of God, a beloved child of God, little children in the same family as our older brother Jesus, the child of God incarnate. It is the image that Jesus chooses for himself and that the gospels reveal: Jesus is the beloved child and son of God. God is his father.

In light of the past understanding of children, the call to become children is startling. It is a call to become virtually powerless. Jesus' call shows no esteem for power the way society and the world define power. If children then and now

have no power, no rights, no guarantee of survival or love —
and yet are the hopeful and potent possibility for a future —
then they can be dangerous and/or they can be ignored. After
all, even the disciples of Jesus didn't want to be bothered with
children. They too had to learn the sensitivity of Jesus and
the wisdom in Jesus' choice of who is important in his family
and kingdom on earth. Let us look to scripture for some short
stories of children and of becoming like a child. There we see
what Jesus is saying to adults, both about children and about
how to become childlike.

One of the first stories about children is found in Matthew — the wayward children:

> *"What comparison can I use to describe this breed? They are
> like children squatting in the town squares, calling to their
> playmates:*
>
> > *'We piped you a tune but you did not dance!*
> > *We sang you a dirge but you did not wail!'*
>
> *In other words, John appeared neither eating nor drinking, and
> people say, 'He is mad!' The Son of Man appeared eating and
> drinking, and they say, 'This one is a glutton and drunkard,
> a lover of tax collectors and those outside the law!' Yet time
> will prove where wisdom lies"* (Matthew 11:16-19).

In light of the status of children and how little esteemed
their opinions and behaviors were, Jesus' description of this
generation of Jews — or us — is hardly flattering. These believers reject both the call to repentance and the austerity of
John's message and Jesus' call to feasting with the bridegroom
and the extensive mercy of God. They "squat in the town
squares," thoughtlessly ignoring the prophets and the word
of God, playing games with religion. These believers are not
just children; they are unaware, and unresponsive to any
message that God sends to them. Are we believers in this
generation any better? God's wisdom is often ignored by the
children of this world.

Then, at the end of this same chapter, Jesus must have startled his listeners and disciples again.

*On one occasion Jesus spoke thus: "Father, Lord of heaven and earth, to you I offer praise; for what you have hidden from the learned and the clever you have revealed to the merest children. Father, it is true. You have graciously willed it so. Everything has been given over to me by my Father. No one knows the Son but the Father, and no one knows the Father but the Son — and anyone to whom the Son wishes to reveal him.*

*"Come to me, all you who are weary and find life burdensome, and I will refresh you. Take my yoke upon your shoulders and learn from me, for I am gentle and humble of heart. Your souls will find rest, for my yoke is easy and my burden light" (Matthew 11:25-30).*

What a switch! The wisdom of God belongs to children, merest children, before it belongs to adults, wise in religion and the ways of society and culture. Jesus gives thanks that this is the way God is revealed in the world through him, his own child. Revelation is not first to the learned and clever but to the ones who don't count, the ones ignored in the street, the ones who are only useful as menial servants and slaves, as property. Remember, the Aramaic word for child and slave/ servant is the same.

And yet, Jesus goes on to describe himself as son, a child who has been given everything by his father. All that God has is now his, and he can do what he wants with it — give it freely to whomever he chooses. That choice is not bound by society's and culture's rules and traditions. Jesus' gift of revealing God is and will be extended to whomever he pleases — not necessarily to those who are expecting to get the revelation. In fact, the ones who are invited, called to learn, to know, and to belong to God are all those who are weary and find life burdensome, all those who are poor and downcast, cast aside, those who don't count. The revelation of God, the presence of Jesus is for them first; he comes to refresh them. The command to take his yoke upon our shoulders and learn from him is unlike the yoke of law, of parents who teach by fear, intimidation, abuse, punishment, playing children off against each other, using their children for their own ends and means, so unlike the yoke of society that sees children as useful for menial tasks. The yoke of Jesus is gentle and humble, close to the earth, human and merciful, tender as a mother for a child, a father for a newborn, a grandparent with grandchildren. In this revelation, this relationship, we will find rest, comfort, care, protection, and light-heartedness.

Often in Central American communities people talk about a yoke, since they still use oxen to plow their fields and carry their produce to market and have ox-drawn carts for convenience. When two oxen are placed in the yoke, an older one is paired with a younger, less experienced animal. The older disciplines and keeps drawing the younger one back into the path of the plough or the road. They go two by two, balancing one another. One ox yoked to another in this way can carry great loads for long periods of time. Oxen are docile, hardworking, essential to the people's life and livelihood. The yoke is for service, for obedience and hard work, necessary hard work. Jesus invites us to take a yoke on our shoulders! But Central Americans know and talk about other yokes: the yoke of invasion and occupation, of attacks from other groups, of fear and poverty enforced by outside bans and sanctions, of isolation and separation and no dignity. They would gladly accept the yoke that was gentle and humble of heart instead of the ones they have always known.

This yoke—the word is also used in Middle Eastern languages to connote laying arms on another's shoulders and dancing in circles and long lines. This yoke is familiar, comfortable, companionable, easy and full of delight, music, song, and dance. To be so yoked means friendship, even in the face of hardship and suffering and loss. This yoke is preferable to any other. In old translations of the Bible Jesus was "yoked" to the cross, his burden laid across his shoulders and tied to his back. He carried this yoke to the hill, and it became his cross, his instrument of public execution. He was made to carry and participate in his own humiliation and execution. How can this yoke be easy and the burden light?

And yet, when I mention this in small groups and communities studying the scriptures, there are knowing looks, gentle smiles of understanding, because Central Americans know too of that yoke, of the shared suffering in the struggle for justice, its horror and its gentleness, and how it draws people together and calls forth from them; even strangers, acts of kindness and care, protection and gentleness. They recall how they treat those who suffer for the people with utmost tenderness, as one would a child or a lover. Yes, this yoke is easy and the burden can be light. This small piece of the gospel is one they remember, put to music, pray aloud in hard times, and repeat as a blessing when we leave the village. This piece is remembered and taken to heart, understood, and prayed over and over again in hope. The merest children understand and teach the theologians and the visiting missionaries the depth of the wisdom of God in choosing this way of revelation, this group of insignificant and unlearned people, the poor. These people, these merest children, know the Father. Jesus has chosen to reveal his beloved Father to them, and they pass on the stories and the knowledge and the faith to those who have ears to hear and eyes to see—to anyone who will listen and share their burden.

Again in Matthew, we find this concept of childhood and its importance in Jesus' kingdom even more clearly outlined.

> *Just then the disciples came up to Jesus with the question, "Who is of greatest importance in the kingdom of God?" He called a little child over and stood him in their midst and said: "I assure you, unless you change and become like little children, you will not enter the kingdom of God. Whoever makes himself lowly, becoming like this child, is of greatest importance in that heavenly reign" (Matthew 18:1-4).*

The greatest in the kingdom is the lowest of the lowly. This turns upside down the existing social structure and ideas of power and authority, of influence and wisdom. Jesus singles out the most unlikely, the most forgotten and ignored of people, the most useless in a society that looks upon abilities and contributions to society as critical, and he says that unless we become like this, we will not enter his kingdom. It is a call that does not sanction upward mobility and independence; it calls us to downward mobility and servanthood, to be obedient to everyone.

This call today is often considered demeaning and is rejected fiercely. And yet it is not unheard of or misunderstood in some places. Over a period of seven years I spent much time in northern New Mexico and listened to stories of people who had grown up in small villages and towns. They spoke of their childhood, of belonging to all the adults in the town, known by all, and told by all what to do—when not to do something, to go home, to fetch, and to do errands. They carried water, firewood, and slops, emptied chamber pots, and were sent on errands by their parents, grandparents, and neighbors. But they spoke too of belonging to all the people, of being accepted, cared for, loved, and protected. Home was not a house, but a place of relationships, of extended family, a place that looked out for others' needs and considered it normal for children to obey and serve. When this passage was discussed in small groups, it dawned on the participants that this is childhood in the kingdom—service combined with belonging, obedience given in love, servanthood that is both joyful and hard, expected and appreciated. It revealed a relationship that bound the community tightly together and an atmosphere that shared responsibility and privileges across family ties. It was home.

Jesus' kingdom is an invitation, a command to change and accept this kind of service, obedience, servanthood, and loving community. It is a command to let go of power, prestige, competition, influence, bullying, and ego in favor of giving freely when asked, when needed, and when simply there. It is a call to help others, to serve, and to obey others, to bend before others and see ourselves as useful to others' needs. The greatest in the kingdom of Jesus follows Jesus' lead—responding to the needs of others, forgiving, healing, feeding, comforting, easing, accompanying, and revealing that this is how God the Father mothers and nurtures us all, all the time, no matter our age.

The story in Matthew then continues with a warning:

*"Whoever welcomes one such child for my sake welcomes me. On the other hand, it would be better for anyone who leads astray one of these little ones who believe in me, to be drowned by a millstone around his neck, in the depths of the sea" (Matthew 18:5-6).*

Welcoming a child—this is where it becomes more obvious that Jesus is not just talking about children newly born and up to the age of fifteen, though they are included. Welcoming a child is welcoming Jesus, when that welcome is done for his sake—in obedience to need, in service and kindness, in outgoing love, in presence, in response to requests, in bending to honor. This passage is more clearly defined in Matthew 25, when Jesus tells the parable of the sheep and the goats at the judgment of the nations, when the Son of Man separates all the peoples of the earth into those in the kingdom and those outside of it. The criterion for belonging in the kingdom forever is this: "Whatsoever you do to the least of your brothers and sisters you do to me." That means corporal works of mercy: feeding the hungry, giving drink to the thirsty, healing and visiting the sick, burying the dead, setting the prisoners free, sheltering the homeless, clothing the naked—serving the needs of others as a child would wish to be served and taken care of, freely and with dignity.

The second half of Jesus' warning is clear—to lead astray a little one, to lead astray those in need, the poor, and the helpless, those fallen through the cracks of society and our parishes, is to merit death—a judgment that is harsh and complete, expulsion from the dream of living in the kingdom. What is done here is just repeated and echoed there forever. To lead children—the least in the world according to the world's standards—astray, to contribute to their demise and their destruction and loss of dignity and hope is to do the same to Jesus. Exile from the kingdom is the response of the Son of Man. A child, this son of man, this child of man, this child of humanity, our judge, is God's reflection in humankind. This child who judges is all the poor, the lost, the forgotten, and the forsaken of this world. This child stands before us with God, and together they cast the ballot either in our favor or for our expulsion from their presence forever.

We are all the children of God with Jesus, who is incarnated in our midst and remains with us in the poor and the least and the ones without any power except the allegiance and favor of God. If we are to be at home in this kingdom forever, we must get used to the company here below and make friends with the children of God, especially those without power in society. Jesus goes on:

> "See that you never despise one of these little ones. I assure you, their angels in heaven constantly behold my heavenly Father's face. What is your thought on this: A man owns a hundred sheep and one of them wanders away; will he not leave the ninety-nine out on the hills and go in search of the stray? If he succeeds in finding it, believe me he is happier about this one than about the ninety-nine that did not wander away. Just so, it is no part of your heavenly Father's plan that a single one of these little ones shall ever come to grief" (Matthew 18:10-14).

This parable of the lost and straying sheep we often hear only in the context of ourselves as the individual sheep, the sinner straying from the flock, from the church, but the context here is much broader than that specific situation. The lost and straying sheep is the one not attended to, cared for, or kept in the community. God heads off after the one that no one else cares about or has even noticed is missing. The warning is for us not to despise any of these lost and straying ones—we who are of the ninety-nine that don't stray or get lost or slip through the cracks in society and yet often forget about the one sheep that no one realizes is missing and in need, helpless and vulnerable to the wild and predators. When the lost ones are missing from our churches, our groups, and families, we often despise them, ignore them, and think poorly of them. Jesus is clear—he and God are most mindful of them. He thinks of them before those of us who take care of our own needs. He is harsh in reminding us of those who have strayed, especially those lost because of our carelessness, rejection, or lack of thoughtfulness and protection.

This whole image subverts existing reality and undermines what society says is important, is power, is independence. The upside-down wisdom of the kingdom of God is distressing and can be very disconcerting to many of us who find ourselves securely in the ninety-nine that God has left to go off searching for the lost sheep. If we want to be the greatest in the kingdom, the most holy, the most like Jesus, true disciples, then our way in the world is the care of the lost sheep, the journey into the wilderness, outside the structures of society in order to make sure that the least are well taken care of and provided for. It is a way of holiness that serves, searches out the lost, and leaves behind those who are at ease.

Home is going after the lost, the little ones, the children of God. One old woman, a grandmother of many, told me that if we want to behold the face of God always, we find it in those little ones, the lost, the ones needing to be found, taken in and taken care of, the least, the poor. She knew the wisdom of God and put it bluntly. The face of God looks remarkably like the face of the least of the lost in society, the little ones, beloved, and most favored children in the kingdom that Jesus brings.

In Mark's gospel the belief about childhood in the kingdom appears in the middle section of the gospel—in the midst of the announcement of the passion and death of Jesus and what discipleship entails. Immediately after the second mention of the passion and the cross comes this story:

*They returned to Capernaum and Jesus, once inside the house, began to ask them, "What were you discussing on the way home?" At this they fell silent, for on the way they had been arguing about who was the most important. So he sat down and called the Twelve around him and said, "If anyone wishes to rank first, he must remain the last one of all and the servant of all." Then he took a little child, stood him in their midst, and putting his arms around him, said to them, "Whoever welcomes a child such as this for my sake welcomes me. And whoever welcomes me welcomes, not me, but him who sent me" (Mark 9:33-37).*

The disciples are a group, a select group around Jesus; they travel with him, eat with him, learn to pray the way he does, and are publicly associated with him and his message of the kingdom. The disciples are having a theological discussion as they travel. After hearing the teaching about what is going to happen to the Son of Man, they shift the focus onto themselves, questioning who is the greatest, the most important among them. Ambition and power and position affect even their small group of twelve. When questioned by Jesus, they become silent. So Jesus gathers them and puts a child in their midst. Then he wraps his arms about the child in a gesture of intimacy, closeness, and care, and he tells his competitive disciples that this is how they should be: trusting, insignificant in many ways, dependent, open, receptive, ordinary. Children — the majority of people in the world — are the image of authority, of power, for Jesus' community. Specifically, if we want to be the first, we must remain last and the servant of all — the servant, the one who attends to the needs of all, obedient, watchful, responsive even before being asked, doing what is expected and doing it faithfully, doing it with joy.

This same thought is one of the last that Jesus shares with his friends at the Last Supper, after breaking bread and sharing the cup with them. Even there the disciples end up in an argument:

> *A dispute arose among them about who should be regarded as the greatest. He said: "Earthly kings lord it over their people. Those who exercise authority over them are called their benefactors. Yet it cannot be that way with you. Let the greater among you be as the junior, the leader as the servant. Who, in fact, is the greater — he who reclines at table or he who serves the meal? Is it not the one who reclines at table? Yet I am in your midst as the one who serves you" (Luke 22:24-27).*

The child image is Jesus himself, the servant of all — the one who washes the feet of his friends, the one who waits on the sinner, the one who sets off to seek the lost and carry them back, the one who sides with the poor and the rejects and the refuse of society. Authority is not to be exercised as power, but as service. Bending before the needs of people is not that far removed from bending before God in worship.

It is in Luke that some of the hardest and most pointed remarks are found about children and servants. In fact, sometimes Luke's gospel is called the servant gospel, the gospel of the servant community, or the gospel of the Suffering Servant of God, Jesus.

> *"If one of you had a servant plowing or herding sheep and he came in from the fields, would you say to him, 'Come and sit down at table'? Would you not rather say, 'Prepare my supper. Put on your apron and wait on me while I eat and drink. You can eat and drink afterward'? Would he be grateful to the servant who was only carrying out his orders? It is quite the same with you who hear me. When you have done all you have been commanded to do, say, 'We are useless servants. We have done no more than our duty' "* (Luke 17:7-10).

Devastating, humbling, and annoying at best. Downright rejected by many and heartily disliked by many others. Servants!? Children!? Yes, children and servants like Jesus, the one rejected by the authorities and legally though unjustly sentenced to death by crucifixion for the hope he gave to the poor, the least of the people, the outcasts, the public sinners, and those who slipped through the cracks of a society that kept so many people without dignity and hope. Children and servants freely aligned with Jesus the child and servant. Children and servants bear their share of the burden of the gospel, as Paul tells Timothy. Children and servants are like Mary, the lowly servant who is called blessed by all ages and whose soul magnifies the greatness of the Lord who does great thing for her. This child is one of those who experience God's great goodness: the lowly, the meek, the hungry, the faithful ones who sing with Mary the song of Magnificat. Mary is one of these children, one of these servants of the Lord who live only to obey the word as it is revealed in the history of God's people. She is blessed; she trusts that the word of God will be fulfilled; she sings on behalf of all these children of God who have long awaited their salvation, their freedom, their being singled out for the love of God. These are the children, the servants who treasure these things, these words in their hearts, realizing that God has heard them, taken note of them, and is on their side. In fact, God is attached to them and hears them first, looking out for them before taking note of the others. What a change for them!

Perhaps the segment of the gospels that is alluded to most often in this context of children is related in Mark 10:13-16 and in Luke 18:15-17.

> *People were bringing their little children to him to have him touch them, but the disciples were scolding them for this. Jesus became indignant when he noticed it and said to them: "Let the children come to me and do not hinder them. It is to just such as these that the kingdom of God belongs. I assure you that whoever does not accept the reign of God like a little child shall not take part in it." Then he embraced them and blessed them, placing his hands on them (Mark 10:13-16).*

In Luke there are a few details that are different and significant:

> *They even brought babies to be touched by him. When the disciples saw this, they scolded them roundly; but Jesus called for the children saying: "Let the little children come to me. Do not shut them off. The reign of God belongs to such as these. Trust me when I tell you that whoever does not accept the kingdom of God as a child will not enter into it" (Luke 18:15-17).*

These passages are found in the segments on what is necessary for discipleship—the practice of the virtue of poverty and the taking up of one's cross and denying one's very self. It is the idea of making oneself small, a servant, not noticeable or having great authority but humble and unobtrusive. In both gospels this encounter among the disciples, the children

and their parents and families, and Jesus is immediately followed by the story of the rich young man or the story of one
of the ruling class who asks: "What must I do to share in
everlasting life?" Jesus points to the virtue of poverty: making
oneself poorer so that the poor might be less poor. The way
of the cross is crowded with children—the poor and those
poor for the kingdom.

Often someone mentions a story about St. Catherine of
Sienna in these discussions about spiritual childhood, poverty,
and authority. It seems on one of the streets in Rome there is
a statue of the saint, barefoot and on her way to the Vatican.
She is shown coming out of the poor district of the city, where
she cared for plague victims and the incurable and the poor.
She would go back and forth between the poor, the least of
the city of Rome, and the pope in the Vatican. Her work and
love and service of the poor, which was a result of her mys-
tical relationship with Jesus, the crucified one, gave her the
authority and power to approach the Vatican, the highest
source of power and authority in the church. She called it
back to the gospel, to the virtue and practice of poverty, and
to its true position as a child of God, a servant of the church,
and of the poorest. It is interesting to note that the poor did
not know that she was on her way to the Vatican. They only
knew her as the ministering angel, the visitor who nursed
them, washed them, and treated them as beloved friends and
children. She, too, was one of those children that Jesus
embraced, put his arms around, and held as models for his
disciples.

A child—one who lives at the beck and call of others—has
enormous amounts of energy, spontaneity, and interest in life.
Children are curious, experimental and nonjudgmental, until
they are taught the difference between races, religions, and
economic realities. Everything is very concrete to them; experience is close, intimately connected to them and what is done
to them or what others think about them. They are honest,
the truth-tellers of the world. They know what is going on
and talk about it to anyone and everyone. They will pass
along anything they hear others saying. They endure. They
want to live, to grow up, and to become like someone they

admire or respect or love. They can be easily lost, forgotten about, shunted aside, ignored, or hurt. They are unique and singular but unconscious of their individuality, and often it is very hard for them to express their differences. Without a family they will bond together in groups and gangs in order to belong and to learn how to cope and survive in the face of harshness and loss. It is hard to be a child in the world, and it is just as hard to be a child of God in the world — but it has its blessings and gifts as well.

Our God became human, became a child and dwelled among us. The birth story in Luke is an announcement by angels to shepherds in the field (definitely in the children category). They are told that they will find the child "lying in a manger, wrapped in swaddling clothes" (Luke 2:12, 16). This passage has echoes in the Hebrew scriptures, especially the book of Wisdom:

> In swaddling clothes and with constant care I was
>     nurtured.
> For no king has any different origin or birth,
>     but one is the entry into life for all; and in one the
>     same way they leave it (Wisdom 7:4-6).

This passage is about our common humanity, our mortality, our vulnerability — now shared by God, the Son of Man, the Son of the most High, the son of Mary. But there is another reference that is often forgotten or overlooked. It is about Jerusalem and Jerusalem's unfaithfulness. At your birth "your navel cord was not cut; you were neither washed with water nor anointed, nor were you rubbed with salt, nor swathed in swaddling clothes" (Ezekiel 16:4). Swaddling clothes symbolize constant care, tender regard, nurturing, and attention. Jesus begins as loved, as attended to, and cared for, first by Mary and Joseph, then by shepherds and astrologers and angels, and then by his father God and the Spirit. At Jesus' baptism and transfiguration it is the voice of God that announces and tells those who can hear: "This is my beloved son, child, listen to him, upon him my favor rests!" Being such a child is living in a relationship of trust, of affirmation, of nurture and belovedness, and it can be dangerous — as noted in the story of the slaughter of the innocents of Bethlehem and Jerusalem and in the world today.

Jesus is concerned that his disciples, his community, begin to think in terms of not being great in the world's estimation, not being terribly significant and outstanding, not being "somebody" as the world acknowledges somebody: with influence, authority, knowledge, connections, power, prestige, and reputation. His brothers and sisters are to be available to all, to obey the will of God, to serve, to be sent to others, outsiders, and to draw them in. They are to welcome and care for the least, and so care for God hidden in the world. When the disciples' ambition and envy surfaces they are acting like children, spoiled children, wayward children, not children of the way.

Those who are great in the kingdom don't seek greatness. They are good at being unnoticed; they are generous and gracious and quiet about such actions. Those who are great suffer the way of the cross, take up their cross, or help shoulder another's burden. They show greatness by forgiving, understanding, being merciful, faithful, enduring and meek, nonviolent and attentive to the needs of those worse off. They defer to others in all things that are not definitive in the world. They let God love them, choose them, care for them, embrace them, and call them into the divine presence. They respond gratefully, thankfully to others because of what God has done for them.

To become truly great we must find ourselves in the company of the poor, the suffering, the people of the beatitudes, the woman Mary who sings alone on a hill with an old barren woman now pregnant and two children who will turn the power and authority of the world on its ear. We must join the company of Jesus, the suffering beloved servant of God, who calls us to love one another as God as loves us. We must find ourselves in the company of children, giving ourselves away graciously and unconditionally to all in imitation of the wondrous love of God's child among us. We are in the company of children when we swaddle the world and those who need nurturing and attention. We are in that company of children when we learn servanthood and how to obey the word of God and sing in the company of other children — old, unborn, pregnant, poor, from the back country towns, in occupied territory, waiting for dreams to come true in their lifetime, and doing all in their power to bring justice to those who suffer innocently, unnecessarily, and unjustly. The child who trusts in God and is humble has the quality of a baby: "Like a weaned child on my mother's lap, so is my soul within me" (Psalm 131:2). Our God is childlike, vulnerable in a manger, running from ruthlessness, growing up in an-out-of-the-way place, off the beaten path, in a neighborhood not known for what it produced. He became the suffering servant of God, obedient even unto death on a cross. The face of our God is like this kind of child.

Peter exhorts his community: "Be as eager for milk as new-born babies — pure milk of the spirit to make you grow unto salvation, now that you have tasted that the Lord is good" (1 Peter 2:2-3). Like babies we need to feed on the word of the Lord regularly. This food, this hunger that will never go away and never be completely filled, must start early in the community of Jesus — with baptism and the taste of salt and water, and then on the chewable substance of the scriptures. A starvation diet won't help us to grow up spiritually or mature as adult children of the God of justice, mercy, and peace. God's forgiveness, never-ending and always being offered, makes life sweet and rich and full of hope, calling us to grow up to the full stature of Christ. What do we want to be when we grow up? Children! — like the Christ, the son of the living God; like Elizabeth's child, the prophet John; like the servant of the Lord, Mary the mother of Jesus; like Joseph, the just man who sides with an unborn child that is not his and adopts God into his family. Peter's words become reality. The taste of the goodness of God grows on us, along with servanthood and being the beloved child of God.

What are the characteristics of a child of God? God's children show an imagination and creativity born of the Spirit to tackle any problems that might arise personally and communally and historically. They see the truth of both suffering and goodness in the world, and they speak up on behalf of those who suffer and side with goodness for all. They suffer and are dependent, even helpless in the face of evil, but innocent of evil as well, relying on the presence of God, the Suffering Servant Jesus for company and strength. God's children are utterly sincere and love for the sake of loving, as God is loving. They express needs, emotions, and affections but do not put them before the needs and feelings of others in the community. They are intimately connected to family and community as blood and water kin, and they are aware of others' needs and responsive to them. They share everything, joys and sorrows, lacks and riches, wisdom and endurance with others and hoard nothing for themselves.

Little things matter. Someone once said that resurrection is in the details. Little people matter too, and hope waits and sleeps in little people's lives. The scriptures say we are children of God. Even if we didn't have a good childhood, we can still have one with God; we can listen to the stories of God about being children in the kingdom. We can know the excitement and anticipation of the kingdom coming among us now and believe in wonder and awe the fact that life can end happily ever after. The stories of God are for the children of God, the servants of God, the least in the world. No matter what is going on in the world, there can be stillness and the awareness of the presence of God with us. We are the children of the Maker, the Creator, and the Sustainer of life. As the children of this Trinity we are called to make, create, and sustain life, especially the life of the weak, other children. Jesus is clear with his disciples and us: Let the children come and do not hinder them, do not keep them from me. This is a two-part command: let them come, and do not hinder. The root word for hinder is the same word as Satan—the one who hinders, blocks, and stops. Jesus rarely uses that word because of its strength and power and connotations. The biggest problem with children in the church and the world is us. Children learn from adults, from us. The real quality of church is found in our children, and they can indict us because of what we say and do and do not say and do. The children, the poor, the least among us reach out to Jesus, and often we are standing in the way!

Jesus touched the children. We have to touch the children and touch them often in public, in the presence of others, touch that is safe, ritual, in church, in community so that they can grow up and become human. We need to bless, touch, forgive, embrace, heal, hold, and play with the children and not hide from our need to become whole. We must remember that the children are already in the kingdom; it already belongs to them. Children, of necessity, are already in it; they are the image of God. We are the ones that must be careful. Chronologically Christianity is a religion of adults, not children. But we must become children, baptized in the freedom of the church, of the Trinity and the community, and we must be careful to be what we proclaim to be as witnesses to the presence of God among us, especially in relation to the children, the least, the poor, and the straying and lost sheep. These little ones are the privileged place of revelation for believers, the reminder of God's nearness and gentleness and vulnerability and love. These little ones lead us into the kingdom.

Children are hard to teach. They watch and criticize and become like the adults with whom they grow up. But the problem is with us, with the adult children of God who refuse to grow up and want only to be taken care of rather than do the will of God and do justice and practice mercy and take care of the poor. We whine, cajole, and try to bribe God; we haven't learned how to restore and repair the world. We adult believers need time still to grow up, to become the true children of God. Someone once said that the quality of a government or society is in direct proportion to the quality of care provided to its children. If so, many of us are wayward children, squatting in the town square not listening to any of the prophets, finding something to ignore or complain about in anyone who calls us to repentance and conversion.

In *Creating a Just Future* Jürgen Moltmann says:

> This community in time is truly human community if there is justice between the generations and if the "contract between the generations" is observed. In our present situation we need to honor above all the right of the

child and the rights of the coming generations to life, because the children are the weakest links in the chain of generations, and the generations to come still have no voice and therefore become the first victims of present injustice.*

Yet we cannot be literalists and think only of children under the age of fifteen. There are many people we are not to hinder from the kingdom: anyone who has no access to the existing system or no power to change the system or even to get his or her rights now, the unborn and those who carry them in their womb, those without health care, the young, the single and pregnant, the homeless, the jobless, the under-employed, the elderly, the sick, those cast out because of disease, gender, sexuality, and associations, the mentally ill and physically handicapped, the imprisoned and ex-prisoners — the masses of the people in the world. Jesus tells his disciples not to hinder them and to go out of their way to help them get to Jesus. He touched them, blessed them, and stopped all else that he was doing to pay attention to these people. St. Teresa of Avila's prayer sums it up: You are the body of Christ, and I only have your hands now to touch others; I only have your feet now to go forth to the poor; I only have your body now to embrace those in the world in need of love.

We are the body of Christ, and we are the children of God, servants of God. With Jesus we must touch those left untouched in our societies. After all, as one black woman in a community I lived in for a while said: "How's God gonna take care of all these children if we don't help him with our arms and comfort?" We must begin with the children and all those who are little and not important in the world. When we make decisions we must, as the Native Americans remind us, remember those to come in the next seven generations, and only then may we act.

God borrows our words, our arms and bodies, our hearts and structures and actions to take care of the children, to extend the kingdom and the reign of God. God needs us.

*Jürgen Moltmann, *Creating a Just Future* (London: SCM, 1989), p. 2.

When Jesus talks about children, he talks about how we are to live in the kingdom. When Jesus talks about children he is reminding us that we have the same relationship to God that he does—we are the beloved children of God. We must be adult children of God and take responsibility for the world, the earth, and all the children everywhere. The face of God is most easily seen and loved in the children. "Lord, he got so many!" Are we found among this number? Are we at home yet?

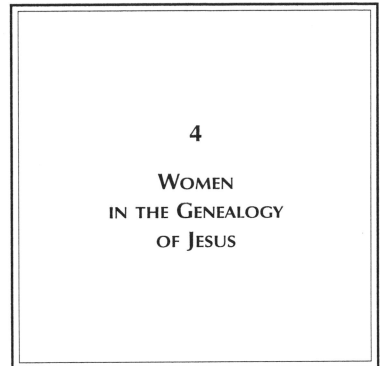

# 4

## WOMEN
## IN THE GENEALOGY
## OF JESUS

L    ike all of us, Jesus the Christ, son of David, son of Abraham, has a history, a record of his ancestors. Since the book and television special *Roots*, many of us have become interested in tracing our own heritages and filling in the branches of our family trees. We want to know who came before us. We need continuity, and we want to see where we fit in a larger picture of the human race. For many, knowing their genealogy provides crucial information on health, disease, patterns of behavior, and modes of death. It provides a sense of identity, a name, a reason for being where and what we are. It ties us to moments of glory and moments of infamy. Our stories are as much about those who have come before us, generated us, and provided us with values and heritages as well as about our own present. Collecting names, relations, and blood and love ties in a genealogy validates our existence and tells us we belong, we issue forth from others. It reminds us that the future is intimate with the past—and that we are the link that holds past and future together.

Jesus' genealogy traces Jesus' Davidic lineage through Joseph, who is called "the husband of Mary." The genealogy overlaps with the very human realities of these people, going all the way back to Abraham. It shows the presence of God Yahweh with these people, people chosen through the covenant and the promises of the Messiah and the hope of justice and peace in the kingdom to come.

The form of Jesus' genealogy is an artificial construct, three sets of fourteen names each, a mnemonic device used because most of this tradition was kept orally. The names come primarily from the books of Genesis, Ruth, 1 Chronicles, and 2 Kings—books many of us are not familiar with. Generally speaking, people are remembered in the Hebrew scriptures for their faithfulness or lack of faithfulness to the covenant and their subsequent relationship to the people. Like anyone's ancestry, it shows a motley crew with some folks to brag about, ancestors anyone would be proud to be associated with or named for, and others that most people would be tempted to erase or conveniently leave out because of their behavior. Jesus' ancestors have a wild and checkered history. The genealogy is in itself a shorthand record of the history of the patriarchs and kings in their long wait for the one who is to come, and everything in history, the bad and the good and the mediocre, is woven into the reality that brings forth Jesus, the Christ, the son of David, the son of Abraham, the adopted son of Joseph, the son of Mary.

It is this last piece that provides startling insights into the story and how it is to be remembered, told, and interpreted. The genealogy is primarily told through the fathers and sons — their lineage — and yet a Jew is a Jew through the mother's blood. Mary, of course, is the closing piece of the story, the edge, the jumping-off place into the reality of Jesus that changes all of history. We read: "Jacob was the father of Joseph the husband of Mary. It was of her that Jesus who is called the Messiah was born" (Matthew 1:16). With that statement the bridge to Jesus is thrown across the years. But the genealogy is patriarchal, and in that tradition it was unheard of to include a woman, let alone end with one. What is even more disconcerting is that not only is Mary mentioned, but four other women as well. They are almost breaks, interruptions in the listing of the men. They stand out and shout to be noticed and certainly to be questioned: Why are you in there? What did you do? Who are you that you are remembered and included in an account that does not usually recognize the power and presence of women in a lineage and tradition except as connected to men, to power, to kings, or in infamy and unfaithfulness? How did you get into Jesus' genealogy? And perhaps the deeper question, What is your connection or what do you have in common with Mary — she of whom the Messiah was born? How are you not only ancestors but sisters to the mother of Jesus? What does your inclusion say to the disciples of Jesus, the community, and the church that comes after you? Who should we be remembering, including and excluding, relying on, boasting about or being ashamed of in our own religious traditions since Jesus' life and death and resurrection? Let's look at these women and see who they are and then try to figure out why their stories are worth singling out for study and hope.

## Tamar

*A family record of Jesus Christ, son of David, son of Abraham. Abraham was the father of Isaac, Isaac the father of Jacob, Jacob the father of Judah and his brothers.*

*Judah was the father of Perez and Zerah, whose mother was Tamar (Matthew 1:1-3).*

Tamar's story is found in chapter 38 of Genesis — way back in the early beginnings of faith's history in the children of Abraham.

*About that time Judah parted from his brothers and pitched his tent near a certain Adullamite named Hirah. There he met the daughter of a Canaanite named Shua, married her, and had relations with her. She conceived and bore a son, whom she named Er. Again she conceived and bore a son, whom she named Onan. Then she bore still another son, whom she named Shelah. They were in Chezib when he was born.*

*Judah got a wife named Tamar for his first-born, Er. But Er, Judah's first-born, greatly offended the LORD: so the LORD took his life. Then Judah said to Onan, "Unite with your brother's widow, in fulfillment of your duty as brother-in-law, and thus preserve your brother's line." Onan, however, knew that the descendants would not be counted as his; so whenever he had relations with his brother's widow, he wasted his seed on the ground, to avoid contributing offspring for his brother. What he did greatly offended the LORD, and the LORD took his life too. Thereupon Judah said to his daughter-in-law Tamar, "Stay as a widow in your father's house until my son Shelah grows up" — for he feared that Shelah also might die like his brothers. So Tamar went to live in her father's house (Genesis 38:1-11).*

It is amazing how much material and time passes in just a
paragraph or two! Judah, the eldest brother of the twelve sons
of Jacob, the one who keeps his other brothers from killing
Joseph in the desert and instead has them sell him into slavery, goes on with his life after lying to his aging father, Jacob.
He marries a Canaanite, they have three sons, and he gets a
wife for his oldest son—Tamar. We really know nothing about
Tamar except that her husbands, the first two sons of Judah,
greatly offended God and so they died and left her doubly
widowed. She is a woman caught in a society's system, married into it. The Jews believed in the "levirate" or "brother-
in-law" marriage, an arrangement that both continued the
line of a deceased son and provided for the widow. We do
not know what the first son, Er, did, but the second son was
disobedient to the law, disrespectful of his brother's name and
wife, and so incurred the anger of God and died. Poor Tamar
is banished to her father's house to live as a widow—isolated
and alone, until the third and last son, Shelah, can grow up.
But she really is being shunned and shunted off to her father
because Judah is afraid for his last son—his own line and
future posterity and name. And so, he too breaks the Law by
not taking Tamar into his house and affording her shelter, a
place to belong to the community, and dignity. This is the
background and the history that brackets the story of Tamar.

From this point we begin to see Tamar as a woman, as a
person who decides what to do and how and acts upon her
decisions. She takes risks and is ingenious in her actions to
secure a future and a place for herself in spite of Judah's
disobedience to the law—the law that was given to protect
her.

*Years passed, and Judah's wife, the daughter of Shua, died.
After Judah completed the period of mourning, he went up to
Timnah for the shearing of his sheep, in company with his
friend Hirah the Adullamite. When Tamar was told that her
father-in-law was on his way up to Timnah to shear his sheep,
she took off her widow's garb, veiled her face by covering herself
with a shawl, and sat down at the entrance to Enaim, which
is on the way to Timnah; for she was aware that, although*

*Shelah was now grown up, she had not been given to him in marriage. When Judah saw her, he mistook her for a harlot, since she had covered her face. So he went over to her at the roadside, and not realizing that she was his daughter-in-law, he said, "Come, let me have intercourse with you." She replied, "What will you pay me for letting you have intercourse with me?" He answered, "I will send you a kid from the flock." "Very well," she said, "provided you leave a pledge until you send it." Judah asked, "What pledge am I to give to you?" She answered, "Your seal and cord, and the staff you carry." So he gave them to her and had intercourse with her, and she conceived by him. When she went away she took off her shawl and put on her widow's garb again (Genesis 38:12-19).*

The plot thickens, and the story begins to get very interesting. It sounds like a soap opera, many people respond at this point, laughingly. Indeed it does, and it's the story of salvation history! This woman may be a widow, but she's tired of waiting for a husband, or more to the point, tired of waiting for her rights and a chance at a life, with dignity and children of her own and a place in the community that she deserves. So she pushes events and people onto the path that they originally should have chosen to follow. It is the path of the Law, the path of inclusion of widows, and the path of faithfulness to the covenant. Judah obeys the parts of the Law that are convenient to him and his future, but not hers, and so she deals with him directly, not with his last and youngest son. It is Judah who must be moved, and she sets him up, knowing his behavior and, obviously, his weaknesses as well. She passes herself off as a harlot, a prostitute, but a very sly one; she has him give her pledges to keep until he pays her due. These pledges are vital to his own person, his identity—his name. They reveal who he is, almost as though he had given her a sealed and written document. She has his name and pledge for the future, not just for this one moment.

It is clear that Judah does have every intention of paying and retrieving his belongings. He sends his friend to deliver the kid to the prostitute on the roadside to Enaim and reclaim his pledges, but the Adullamite can't find her. No one has ever heard of her or seen her. The man comes back empty-handed and Judah responds: "Let her keep the things, otherwise we shall become a laughingstock. After all, I did send her the kid, even though you were unable to find her" (Genesis 38:23). For Judah, the matter is done with. He's fulfilled his responsibilities and tried to pay her back and he has a witness—his friend the Adullamite who tried to deliver payment. He's covered, and he goes on with his life, never thinking twice about what he has done. The one thing he wants to make sure of is that he does not become a laughingstock of the community. He has his pride and his reputation and his place in the community; he can't be bothered with one woman he met casually and took as a prostitute. But for Judah a story is just beginning that will change his life and relations and family line forever. He already has a son and another responsibility. He is just unaware of it at the moment. But Tamar knows exactly what she is doing and time will tell.

> About three months later, Judah was told that his daughter-in-law Tamar had played the harlot and was then with child from her harlotry. "Bring her out," cried Judah; "she shall be burned." But as they were bringing her out, she sent word to her father-in-law, "It is by the man to whom these things belong that I am with child. Please verify," she added, "whose seal and cord and whose staff these are." Judah recognized them and said, "She is more in the right than I am, since I did not give her to my son Shelah." But he had no further relations with her.
>
> When the time of her delivery came, she was found to have twins in her womb. While she was giving birth, one infant put out his hand; and the midwife, taking a crimson thread, tied it on his hand, to note that this one came out first. But as he withdrew his hand, his brother came out; and she said, "What a breach you have made for yourself!" So he was called Perez. Afterward his brother came out; he was called Zerah (Genesis 38:24-30).

Thus the story is done, and Tamar disappears, suddenly to reappear in the genealogy of Jesus.

Tamar sets about making Judah obey the law and take responsibility for her and his behavior toward her in the family. She takes a great risk—of being burned to death with her children unborn. But she also has his pledges and some knowledge of the Law and of Judah himself. When confronted with the evidence and reminded of his own behavior and lack of attention to the Law, he accepts her charge and challenge and accepts her and her twin children, who, of course, are inheritors of his name. Judah makes mistakes in fear, but he is basically a decent man and does not demand that the Law be carried out in her regard; he sees himself as guilty as well. The truth rules, the widow is made mother and accepted back into the family, Judah has his lineage and future hope. Out of disaster and breaking the Law and harlotry by both Judah and Tamar comes hope and continuation and children. Even disobedience and unfaithfulness to the covenant and Law, even temple prostitution, manipulation, deception, and incredibly human affairs can serve the Lord of history. From every experience, every event, even aberrations in behavior can fit into the plan of hope and salvation. But still, why is Tamar included in Jesus' genealogy? What is her connection to Mary, the mother of Jesus?

Why is this woman pulled into the history of remembrance for Matthew's community, for the communal identity of Jesus, the Messiah? The genealogy chronicles the men, those whose blood is to be found in the future hope of the people, but this woman's liaison with Judah breaks the pattern, interrupts the line. She becomes bound to Judah and remembered for her relationship with him, rather than with her husbands, his sons. She is not the normal pattern of wife and mother! She brings new life, a shift, something unexpected into the lineage and history. Her whole story is unexpected, an interruption in the story of Joseph, the youngest of the twelve brothers. And her story brings new life, new blood, new understandings of what the covenant, the Law, and the truth of the future might eventually entail.

In a patriarchal structure women bring about change by their actions, choices, and ingeniousness in their relations with men; they are remembered for their breaks in the pattern. They all are breaches in the chain, the blood lines, breaches in history—important ones to note and incorporate into memory. In a tradition that remembers faithfulness and what contributes to the coming of the Messiah and that looks at sexuality, marriage, and generation all in one piece, what makes these grandmothers of God so unique and special and worthy of memory? What do these women all have in common with Mary, the mother of Jesus, the mother of God?

Tamar is a woman caught in the Law and the disobedience of others to that Law, which should make her secure but instead is used to exclude her. She knows that her life and the lives of her future children are more important than the Law, that the Law must be used to serve life. She is a widow with no rights but one: to be given in marriage to her brother-in-law. She intends to rely on that right; it is her life-line. She breaks the Law—engages in prostitution—to make Judah acknowledge that he is breaking the Law with her. She is being treated unjustly—this is oppression on a small scale. She takes a risk and takes what she needs in order to survive—Judah's seal, cord, and staff, that is, his name, his pledges, and thus his protection and acknowledgment of relationship and responsibility for his actions. She says that the Law may be broken to reveal the truth, to correct injustice, and to protect the life of the weak. Having a child is her only hold on Judah in the existing society, and the child itself will validate her tie to Judah and his family. She is very clear about the double standard—it doesn't hold. It is no longer acceptable and so attested to in the scriptures. This woman is a teacher of justice, fairness, righteousness, and human dignity—all those things that the Law is supposed to serve and uphold. She reveals Judah's hypocrisy, and he admits to it and in turn learns to obey the law. Even wrongdoing is redeemable in Jesus' history. All history is subject to God. And God can work with sinners as easily as saints.

Tamar, like Mary, is a woman alone, pregnant, unmarried, and in jeopardy with the Law. She can be stoned to death along with her unborn child if no one accepts responsibility for the child and the woman in a relationship. Mary must rely on Joseph's righteousness and justice for her very life and the life of her child; the child's birth will validate her life, reveal the truth of history, expose oppression, and right wrong, bring justice, and redeem the situation. Jesus is born out of the ordinary. Mary and Tamar give birth out of the ordinary pattern of life. Obeying the word of God, the spirit of the Law, and breaking the Law can reveal truth, expose oppression, redeem the situation, and bring forth justice. Tamar intimates some of what Mary will experience. Some of the pattern will be repeated, and all of it will be full of grace at the end, revelatory of the truth and justice. The woman and child will be protected.

### Rahab

"Salmon was the father of Boaz, whose mother was Rahab" (Matthew 1:5). Rahab's story is found in the book of Joshua.

*Then Joshua, son of Nun, secretly sent out two spies from Shittim, saying, "Go, reconnoiter the land and Jericho." When the two reached Jericho, they went into the house of a harlot named Rahab, where they lodged. But a report was brought to the king of Jericho that some Israelites had come there that night to spy out the land. So the king of Jericho sent Rahab the order, "Put out the visitors who have entered your house, for they have come to spy out the entire land." The woman had taken the two men and hidden them, so she said, "True, the men you speak of came to me, but I did not know where they came from. At dark, when it was time for the gate to be shut, they left, and I do not know where they went. You will have to pursue them immediately to overtake them." Now, she had led them to the roof, and hidden them among her stalks of flax spread out there. But the pursuers set out along the way to the fords of the Jordan, and once they had left, the gate was shut.*

*Before the spies fell asleep, Rahab came to them on the roof and said: "I know that the LORD has given you the land, that a dread of you has come upon us, and that all the inhabitants of the land are overcome with fear of you. For we have heard how the LORD dried up the waters of the Red Sea before you when you came out of Egypt, and how you dealt with Sihon and Og, the two kings of the Amorites beyond the Jordan, whom you doomed to destruction. At these reports, we are disheartened; everyone is discouraged because of you, since the LORD, your God, is in heaven above and on earth below. Now then, swear to me by the LORD that, since I am showing kindness to you, you in turn will show kindness to my family; and give me an unmistakable token that you are to spare my father and mother, brothers and sisters, and all their kin, and save us from death." "We pledge our lives for yours," the men answered her. "If you do not betray this errand of ours, we will be faithful in showing kindness to you when the LORD gives us the land."*

*Then she let them down through the window with a rope; for she lived in a house built into the city wall. "Go up into the hill country," she suggested to them, "that your pursuers may not find you. Hide there for three days, until they return; then you may proceed on your way." The men answered her, "This is how we will fulfill the oath you made us take: When we come into the land, tie this scarlet cord in the window through which you are letting us down; and gather your father and mother, your brothers and all your family into your house. Should any of them pass outside the doors of your house, he will be responsible for his own death, and we shall be guiltless. But we shall be responsible if anyone in the house with you is harmed. If, however, you betray this errand of ours, we shall be quit of the oath you have made us take." "Let it be as you say," she replied, and bade them farewell. When they were gone, she tied the scarlet cord in the window.*

*They went up into the hills, where they stayed three days until their pursuers, who had sought them all along the road without finding them, returned. Then the two came back down from the hills, crossed the Jordan to Joshua, son of Nun, and reported all that had befallen them. They assured Joshua, "The LORD has delivered all this land into our power; indeed all the inhabitants of the land are overcome with fear of us" (Joshua 2:1-24).*

This is the beginning of Rahab's story—and the story of her entire family. This woman is bound to her mother and father, brothers and sisters, and all of their kin. When she is intent on saving herself, she is intent on saving her family as well. She is a prostitute—she works the walls of the city of Jericho. Her house is built right into the city wall, and as people come and go, she hears all kinds of stories, news, gossip, information. Her house is a passing-through place, and she is privy to all sorts of people, cultures, races, and religious beliefs. She has heard the stories of what God has done for the Israelites and has decided after hearing the word of the Lord and of his saving work, that she will throw in her lot with the Israelites. So she becomes an accessory to the spies, a traitor to her own people, in order to align her family and her future to the people of Israel—the future in the eyes of God. She has a glimpse of what God sees and decides to alter her family's future to be part of the chosen people.

Rahab uses her position, her knowledge, her house, and her influence to save the spies and get them safely back to Joshua. She extracts from them a pledge of life in the midst of the upcoming battle for all her kin. She is to hang a scarlet cord in the window of the place where she lets them down in the wall and that symbol—the red cord in the window—will mark her house and she will be saved along with all her relatives. The oath is exchanged—their lives are now connected to her family's life—the red cord a lifeline. The spies tell Joshua about the people of Jericho's fear and all that happened, and Joshua honors the spies' oath to Rahab.

As the Israelites continue the siege of Jericho, the Lord tells Joshua to circle the city for six days with the ark of the covenant and on the seventh day march around the city and blow the horns and shout and the wall of the city will collapse. Joshua and his soldiers and people obey God, and the battle begins. Joshua is specific in his commands:

"Now shout, for the LORD has given you the city and everything in it. It is under the LORD's ban. Only the harlot Rahab and all who are in the house with her are to be spared, because she hid the messengers we sent" (Joshua 6:16-17).

The shouts bring down the wall and the city is attacked. Then Joshua directs the spies:

> *"Go into the harlot's house and bring out the woman with all her kin, as you swore to her you would do." The spies entered and brought out Rahab, with her father, mother, brothers, and all her kin. Her entire family they led forth and placed them outside the camp of Israel. The city itself they burned with all that was in it, except the silver, gold, and articles of bronze and iron, which were placed in the treasury of the house of the* LORD. *Because Rahab the harlot had hidden the messengers whom Joshua had sent to reconnoiter Jericho, Joshua spared her with her family and all her kin, who continue in the midst of Israel to this day (Joshua 6:22-25).*

From Matthew 1:5 we learn that Rahab married Salmon of the tribe of Judah and thus became the great-great-grandmother of David, Christ's ancestor. One wonders if Salmon was one of the spies!

Rahab lived in rough times, a time of warfare, during the struggle for domination in the promised land after the Exodus. She hears the word of the Lord, the stories of what God does for this people Israel, and she is brought to belief. She leaves her own people and joins with another people and becomes memorable in the history of Israel. A prostitute, she eventually becomes a legitimate wife and mother and grandmother to the greatest king of Israel: David. Thus Rahab, another outsider manages to breach the walls of Israelite history and the lineage of Jesus by her choices, deeds, and craftiness at surviving.

After these two accounts of Tamar and Rahab, perhaps we should look at the way sexuality, marriage, and children were viewed in Israelite society. Many people react with horror to the telling of these stories and ask, "Is nothing sacred?" Their reactions reveal their modern suppositions about sexuality, gender, marriage, and children. The Israelites of our stories are a nomadic people living in hard times and rough terrain. The Law loosely holds them together, and they live the tribal way of life, with alliances and intermarriage. Belonging to a

family, to a line, is survival in the community. Children are a
necessity, a lifeline for parents and a fulfillment of the promise
God made to Abraham that his people and nation would be
great. Sexuality is intimately connected to children, marriage,
the future, the survival of the people. It is not an individual
affair, a psychological relationship. It is tribal, communal, and
connected to procreation; it holds the people together and
gives them an identity in intricate patterns that work, that
sustain life, and that enable people to live together.

Temple prostitution is connected with the worship and the
temple structures of other religions, and prostitution on a
small-time basis exists with women connected to a particular
place or shrine—much like the one that Judah thinks he
encounters on his trip to shear the sheep. Thus Judah not
only engaged in prostitution, but prostitution that was connected to the worship of alien gods—a double infraction of
the Law. Nonetheless, his acknowledgment of his child is
acceptable to the community, as is Tamar's behavior. It is considered understandable in her circumstances. It is not helpful
to view it from the point of view of modern behavior and
approaches to sexuality. This is not to say that what she did
was not wrong, but in these cases especially the behavior must
be seen and understood in the concept of the Law, the covenant, the people, and the future of Israel and the family's
identity and survival.

Rahab, who may have been a prostitute, hears the word of
the Lord, responds, and saves her family. She becomes a vital
part of the Israelite nation, as well as great-great-grandmother
to David and an ancestor to Jesus, a kindred soul to Mary his
mother. Rahab harbors and aids spies, messengers of God. She
puts her own life and family in danger and saves them. Sur-
prisingly, she has a relationship with the existing king—they
write letters back and forth and her explanation to him is
believed and acted upon. She uses her relationships, her reputation, and her lifestyle to help the Israelite people and so
serve the plan of God for his people in her land. In return,
she is included in the covenant. She believes the witnesses to
the history of Israel, the struggling and fledgling Israel, and

acts to ensure her place with them. She risks and finds a way to further the will of God.

The place where God enters Jericho is through a wall in the city, through her house and her actions. The whole story is reminiscent of the Exodus and Passover of the Israelites themselves. Her house is marked with a sign that will allow death to pass over; her family is saved. There is always laughter and delight among discussion groups at the sign—the red cord in the window that has become the red-light district in any city today. Everything can be put to use by the Spirit to serve its own purposes. Nothing is exempt from the power of God and the eventual coming true of God's promises, albeit in remarkable ways.

So there is another breach in history. Sexuality is not the issue here; it is not the primary focus of Rahab. However, in the genealogy and, repeatedly in these women's lives, sexuality—no matter how it is experienced, used, or abused— serves only as one of many experiences that bring forth the Messiah and contribute to the will of God made flesh in history. The issue in this woman's life is her hearing of the word of God from messengers foreign to her and her response: "Let it be as you say"—the words are almost an exact duplication of Mary's word to the angel: "Be it done to me as you say" or "Be it done unto me according to your word." The connection is clear. Sexuality is not a primary criterion in responding to and hearing the word of the Lord and acting upon it to make it come true in reality, even in dangerous circumstances for the women involved. Rahab cares about her family, her kin, and she does what she can and must to save her people. She throws in her lot with the children of Israel, and she is accepted and taken in as family. Her courage and a scarlet cord bind the spies to their word and to Israel, and she will live with honor in Israel for her part in the battle and the coming into the promised land. She begins by taking in and caring for the messengers of God, believing their words and stories, and acting to make that word a reality in her life and the world. Mary and Rahab are definitely soul-sisters, intent on the same thing in difficult times. The pattern draws these women closer and closer.

## Ruth

Ruth is one of the most widely known and loved women in the Hebrew scriptures though she is also often misunderstood. Ruth too is an outsider who marries in, and yet she is not remembered for her marriages, but for her friendship with an older woman, her mother-in-law Naomi. The words we often used in marriage ceremonies today—"Wherever you go, I will go ..."—were not spoken to a husband-to-be, but to her mother-in-law. Both women had been left alone and bereft, without connection to the society and a man's family. Ruth's story is one of solidarity between women; it tells how two women work together and use their wits and their love to survive and become part of a people as well as most remarkable friends. Ruth's story is found in her own book and her name appears in the genealogy in the line following Rahab's:

*Boaz was the father of Obed, whose mother was Ruth.*
*Obed was the father of Jesse*
*Jesse the father of King David (Matthew 1:5-6).*

Ruth's story begins in Bethlehem in a time of famine. A man departs from there to reside in Moab. The man is Elimelech and his wife is Naomi and his sons are Mahlon and Chilion. Soon Elimelech dies, leaving Naomi a widow. Her two sons marry Moabite women, one named Orpah and the other Ruth. After ten years both the men die, leaving another two women widowed. Naomi decides to go back to Bethlehem because she has heard that the Lord has visited his people and given them food. She entreats both her daughters-in-law to return to their mother's houses and to seek with her blessing for husbands and children for the future. Twice she pleads with them, for she has nothing, her lot is bitter, and she would not wish it on her daughters-in-law. Orpah kisses her goodbye and leaves, but Ruth decides to stay with her. It is Ruth's answer that is so well remembered:

*"See now!" she [Naomi] said, "your sister-in-law has gone back to her people and her god. Go back after your sister-in-*

law!" But Ruth said, "Do not ask me to abandon or forsake
you! for wherever you go I will go, wherever you lodge I will
lodge, your people shall be my people, and your God my God.
Wherever you die I will die, and there be buried. May the LORD
do so and so to me, and more besides, if aught but death
separates me from you!" Naomi then ceased to urge her, for
she saw she was determined to go with her.

So they went on together till they reached Bethlehem. On
their arrival there, the whole city was astir over them, and the
women asked, "Can this be Naomi?" But she said to them,
"Do not call me Naomi. Call me Mara, for the Almighty has
made it very bitter for me. I went away with an abundance,
but the LORD has brought me back destitute. Why should you
call me Naomi, since the LORD has pronounced against me
and the Almighty has brought evil upon me?" Thus it was
that Naomi returned with the Moabite daughter-in-law, Ruth,
who accompanied her back from the plateau of Moab. They
arrived in Bethlehem at the beginning of the barley harvest
(Ruth 1:15-22).

Ruth refuses to leave her mother-in-law. She casts her lot
with her because of friendship and love. If she returns to her
own people, she can marry again, but if she goes with Naomi,
there is no one in Naomi's line left to marry. She accepts the
hard fate that Naomi herself must live with—being a widow
without children and so living at risk in the community. So
in caring for her mother-in-law and standing in solidarity
with her friend and companion Naomi, Ruth abandons her
country, her religion, her god, and the possibility of being
accepted back into society. In many aspects she abandons her
future for a present that will be full of hardship and poverty
and being an outcast in Bethlehem—a foreigner, one who
does not belong and is not protected by the Law, except as
one of the *anawim,* one of the very poor. Her friendship and
love is full of piety and faithfulness, rare in those days, rare
among many of us today. The words often repeated as part
of the marriage vows were originally an oath transferring allegiance. Ruth was opting to side with someone poorer than
herself, and she spoke with passion and devotion to a friend—

which perhaps is a very good definition of marriage after all!

Naomi and Ruth find themselves in the position of needing to glean the fields of anyone who will allow them to do so — it is their means of survival. The Law required that after the first cutting of a harvest the fields be left to the poor, widows, aliens, foreigners, and strangers to glean before a second harvest or cutting was done. This allowed those with nothing to survive — to eat and sustain their life day to day. Ruth, being younger and stronger, gleans for herself and Naomi, and Naomi suggests that she do it in Boaz's field, since Boaz is a prominent kinsman of her husband Elimelech's clan.

Ruth works hard all day, and when Boaz comes to the field, he notices her and asks his overseer who she is. When he hears of her relationship to Naomi, he goes to her and tells her to glean only in his fields and to stay with his women servants. He suggests how to glean better, commands that she not be harmed by the men, and orders his people to give her water. He does this for her because of what she has done for Naomi, and he prays that the Lord will reward her for what she has done. He says: "May the LORD reward what you have done. May you receive a full reward from the LORD, the God of Israel, under whose wings you have come for refuge" (Ruth 2:12). Ruth responds: "May I prove worthy of your kindness, my lord: you have comforted me, your servant, with your consoling words; would indeed that I were a servant of yours!" (Ruth 2:13). Later he allows her to eat with him and his harvesters and allows her to glean even among the sheaves rather than just among the stubble. He even orders his harvesters to drop some handfuls of grain for her. So Ruth remains in Boaz's fields gleaning, and Naomi blesses her kinsman for his kindness.

Then the story shifts. Naomi does some thinking and comes up with a strategy. She suggests to Ruth:

> *"My daughter, I must seek a home for you that will please you. Now is not Boaz, with whose servants you were, a relative of ours? This evening he will be winnowing barley at the threshing floor. So bathe and anoint yourself; then put on your best attire and go down to the threshing floor. Do not make*

*yourself known to the man before he has finished eating and drinking. But when he lies down, take note of the place where he does so. Then go, uncover a place at his feet, and lie down. He will tell you what to do." "I will do whatever you advise," Ruth replied. So she went down to the threshing floor and did just as her mother-in-law had instructed her (Ruth 3:1-6).*

Naomi knows Ruth well and treats her as a daughter. She knows Boaz from his previous care of Ruth and his kindness to herself in providing for them. So she devises this way for Ruth to introduce a claim on Boaz—for Boaz to obey the law of Deuteronomy and both reclaim lost land for an impoverished widow as well as take Ruth as his wife. Ruth follows Naomi's directions to the letter and finds where Boaz sleeps and sleeps at his feet. He awakens in the middle of the night and discovers her; they speak and together they plan on how to be married. Boaz must make some arrangements and deal with another who has prior claim to the land, but he promises that he will do all that he can to claim her as his wife. Then he gives her six measures of barley to bring back to Naomi and protects her reputation among his own men and harvesters.

Boaz goes to the city gate and intercepts the man with the prior claim and is given leave to acquire the land that once belonged to Elimelech and also to take Ruth as his wife. The elders at the gate are the witnesses and give the blessing:

*"We do so. May the LORD make this wife come into your house like Rachel and Leah, who between them built up the house of Israel. May you do well in Ephrathah and win fame in Bethlehem. With the offspring the LORD will give you from this girl, may your house become like the house of Perez, whom Tamar bore to Judah" (Ruth 4:11-12).*

So, we are told, Boaz takes Ruth and Ruth bears a child, an heir. This time it is the women who bless Naomi:

*"Blessed is the LORD who has not failed to provide you today with an heir! May he become famous in Israel! He will be your*

*comfort and the support of your old age, for his mother is the*
*daughter-in-law who loves you. She is worth more to you than*
*seven sons!" (Ruth 4:14-15).*

Naomi's grandson was named Obed, and he was the father
of Jesse, the father of David.

And now Ruth and Naomi are given back to history, to
resurface in the genealogy connected to Jesus. The connections are easily made. Ruth sides with Naomi and gives her
life to Naomi in love and friendship, leaving everything to
make her mother-in-law's life easier. She pledges her life even
unto death to her. She sides with and lives in solidarity with
a poor woman in a foreign country and takes on another race,
another nation, another religion, and another's blood ties. She
hands over any independence or life she could have had so
that another might not be totally abandoned in her need.
They are both poor, fending for themselves, but they are not
helpless; they share love, history, and hope together. Naomi
is in need, but Ruth's situation is worse because she is an
outsider. Yet this outsider comes to teach Israel what true
faithfulness and love is and can be. Though they have no
security, no income, they do have a plan for survival. They
work together so that both of them can live and have a future.
They use all the resources they have, including family connections, to change their position in society, to marry, even
to marry for love to some degree, and to raise up children.
Ruth's unselfish love becomes the image of love and faithfulness not only in friendship but marriage and family, and
among a people she is the image of single-hearted devotion
to the poor.

I have often heard this section of the book of Ruth used to
promise faithfulness among missionaries when they commit
themselves to a people until death. They promise to accompany them on their journey and share their life and struggles
and hopes with this kind of devotion and single-heartedness.
Ruth's generosity, her honorableness even in poverty, her
dignity and her choice, her options and obedience to another's even more desperate need, and her love win her a place
in Jesus' family tree. Her charity and her mercy makes her

memorable. This grandmother to God teaches faithfulness, tender-hearted love, and hard-headed attention to life. Some say that she is the one of the first to make the option for the poor.

Ruth and Mary are kindred souls, revealing the ways of God. They both hand over their independence to God, promising their lives to serve another's life. They both are incredibly faithful to that word. They both give over their life and will to God's will in history and in their stories. Much of what Mary sings about in the Magnificat—of her lowliness and servanthood and obedience and love and glory—is done for the poor and the oppressed. She is one of that group that echoes Ruth's life and connection to Naomi and then to Boaz and Bethlehem's people. Ruth and Naomi conspire together for a future hope. Remember the word *conspire* means "to breathe together." Mary and Elizabeth and the Spirit conspire again to bring forth children. Again two women, one old and barren and one unmarried and pregnant, will conspire together with God to bring forth children who will be great in Israel. Elizabeth, who endured the slander of her own people because she bore no children, and Mary, who endured the same slander and the possibility of death because she was pregnant, together rejoice and together help each other in friendship, love, and faithfulness.

Kinship by blood and spirit and love is how the story of Jesus begins. It has happened before and been remembered. The story is situated in Bethlehem, beginning in famine and ending in feasting and in the fields of barley. The whole city is astir when Naomi and Ruth return home. Once again Bethlehem will be astir when news of the child comes with the magi on their visit to Herod, but for different reasons. The man Boaz takes care of the widow, the foreigner in his midst, with kindness, and this has always been the criteria for faithfulness in Israel. Another man will echo this kindness and protection, the just man Joseph, who for love and faithfulness will take Mary and a child into his house and marry her and adopt the child. And what will come forth from this child, Jesus, will be the light of the world, greater by far than David, the king of old.

Ruth is truly a woman of valor. She is a woman who puts another woman, older and in need, first in her life. She is a friend to an elder, her mother-in-law, revealing love that is different than love of man for woman, husband for wife, but love, true and serving of the will of God, the love of a friend. Even her child with Boaz was seen as a gift for Naomi, a grandchild who brought her blessing and happiness in her old age. The women themselves announce that this woman friend and daughter Ruth is worth more than seven sons! This kind of love, of affection and service, of solidarity is a rare gift, one that will echo God's love for his friends. These women travelers together make a hard history lovely to behold. They have to scrounge and be scavengers and folks on the fringe, but they share more than a hunger for food. Their friendship is stronger than any fear or reality that they have to endure. They stay together and carve out a way, a new way that is recognized as good.

Mary and Elizabeth know that friendship. Mary goes to Elizabeth in haste, to hill country outside of Jerusalem for solace, for protection, for knowledge from an older woman. She will learn from her how it is to be pregnant, how to birth, and how to have the courage to return to her own village of Nazareth three months pregnant. Elizabeth will recognize Mary for who she is, not just poor and pregnant but the mother of the Messiah, the long-awaited one. Mary is courageous enough to stake her life on the word of God, to have no life but the life that the word of God wills, and Elizabeth will bless Mary as the one who believed and trusted and so brought to life the Word in her flesh, who brought forth the Word into history in a child, and who loved in ways that were different.

Mary and Elizabeth were friends and Mary and Joseph were friends and loved faithfully, as God loves. Thus new relationships are revealed. Sexuality is not the only basis of love. God relies on friendship as the image of intimacy in the kingdom. Sometimes leftovers, remnants, and those who fall through the cracks in the Law are those who have to make new alliances creatively and imaginatively. They reveal the way God works in the world better than the acceptable ways.

Mary is connected to God the way Ruth and Naomi are bound, and Mary is bound to Joseph as freely and passionately as these two women are friends. God is making friends and opening up possibilities from way back.

### Bathsheba, The Wife of Uriah

The last woman in the genealogy is not named, though we know her well. She appears soon after in history.

*David was the father of Solomon,*
  *whose mother had been the wife of Uriah (Matthew 1:6).*

Why isn't she named as the others are? Again, there is a jump, a glitch, an abnormal interruption in the bloodlines. Jesus does not come from the marriage of David and his other wives and concubines. We are told that David was thirty when he became king in Israel and ruled for forty years. In fact, ten children are named and listed in 2 Samuel 5:13-15. David was great in Israel and beloved by God, but David was not always great or consistently holy and faithful. He has some incredibly good moments and some incredibly bad ones. His evil and his goodness seem almost extremes. David prays and sings the honor and glory of God, serves God, and even wishes to build a house for the ark of the covenant. David wars and seeks to bring his people together into one nation. But he has another side. The story of the woman, the wife of Uriah the Hittite, the woman Bathsheba, begins in a lull between battles. David has sent out his troops and officers, and they are besieging Rabbah, but David has remained behind in Jerusalem.

*One evening David rose from his siesta and strolled about on the roof of the palace. From the roof he saw a woman bathing, who was very beautiful. David had inquiries made about the woman and was told, "She is Bathsheba, daughter of Eliam, and wife of [Joab's armor-bearer] Uriah the Hittite." Then David sent messengers and took her. When she came to him, he had relations with her, at a time when she was just purified after her monthly period. She then returned to her house. But the woman had conceived, and sent the information to David, "I am with child" (2 Samuel 11:2-5).*

Much of what is written in Kings and Samuel is about David the king, but this story is about David the man—and the story is entitled "David's Sin." David sees a beautiful woman, wants her, sends for her, and takes her. She becomes pregnant, and she sends word to David that she is with child. There are two people involved in this conception: David and Bathsheba. Many people who read this story want the story to say that David raped Bathsheba and thus Bathsheba had no choice in the matter. There is certainly that element of power and privilege in her submission to the king. But note that Bathsheba responds to her pregnancy by telling David. She knows—and David knows—that her husband, Uriah, is away on campaign (for David) and there is no way she could be carrying Uriah's child. So she aligns herself with David. Even though she does not participate in the following actions, she may be aware of what is going on. There is no mention of her protesting what is done to her husband. And, of course, she *does* become queen in Israel, the wife of David, and the mother of Solomon.

Many people speculate that her name is not included in the genealogy because she was the wife of Uriah, and it is Uriah's being caught in David's sin and Bathsheba's profit from it that excludes her. She continues the pattern of interruption, but murder and collusion and profit from evil are part of her story.

The story continues. David sends a message recalling Uriah. David tries to get him to go home and see his wife, but Uriah will not. Instead, he stays in the palace. When questioned by David about why he doesn't go home, he responds that the ark of the covenant is lodged in a tent, so how can he go to his home? And so Uriah is sent back to Joab, his commander, with a message that sets him up for death. It reads: "Place Uriah up front, where the fighting is fierce. Then pull back and leave him to be struck down dead" (2 Samuel

11:15). David's plan works, and the word comes back to David that Uriah is dead. The text reads: "When the wife of Uriah heard that her husband had died, she mourned her lord. But once the mourning was over, David sent for her and brought her into his house. She became his wife and bore him a son, but the LORD was displeased with what David had done" (2 Samuel 11:26-27). Now Bathsheba is queen of Israel and lives in David's house. Their child has brought her into marriage.

At this point in the story Nathan the prophet is summoned by God to go to David. Nathan tells David a story about a case that he wants David to judge. It is the story of two men, one rich with many flocks and herds and one with only one poor little ewe lamb. This lamb was like a daughter to him, growing up among his family and children. The rich man received a visitor, but didn't take from his own flock to feed him. Instead, he took the one ewe of the poor man to feed his visitor.

David grows angry and tells Nathan: "As the LORD lives, the man who had done this merits death! He shall restore the ewe lamb fourfold because he has done this and has had no pity" (2 Samuel 12:5-6). David is caught in the trap, and Nathan turns on him:

*"You are the man! Thus says the LORD God of Israel: 'I anointed you king of Israel. I rescued you from the hand of Saul. I gave you your lord's house and your lord's wives for your own. I gave you the house of Israel and of Judah. And if this were not enough, I could count up for you still more. Why have you spurned the LORD and done evil in his sight? You have cut down Uriah the Hittite with the sword; you took his wife as your own, and him you killed with the sword of the Ammonites. Now, therefore the sword shall never depart from your house, because you have despised me and have taken the wife of Uriah to be your wife.' Thus says the LORD: 'I will bring evil upon you out of your own house. I will take your wives while you live to see it, and will give them to your neighbor. He shall lie with your wives in broad daylight. You have done this deed in secret, but I will bring it about in the*

*presence of all Israel, and with the sun looking down'* " *(2 Samuel 12:7-12).*

David acknowledges his sin, and Nathan tells David that he is forgiven and will not die: "But since you have utterly spurned the LORD by this deed, the child born to you must surely die." David beseeches God for the life of the child, but the child grows ill, desperately ill. David fasts, but the child dies seven days later. Then David worships God and comforts his wife, Bathsheba. They come together again, and she again becomes pregnant. The child they have together is Solomon and the Lord loved him, we are told. So Bathsheba, the wife of Uriah, becomes another interruption in the lineage of Jesus.

Bathsheba loses her husband, murdered by David, who becomes her second husband. She loses her first child, and yet is comforted with a second, who is Solomon, one of the greatest of the kings in Israel. Solomon is often referred to as the sign of peace between God and David and Bathsheba and a sign of God's continuing blessing on the house of David. Life can come even out of murder, deceit, unfaithfulness, and adultery! The kingdom of God can overcome any evil, any sin, individual or social. The child given as a comfort becomes a sign of peace, of hope; he ushers in a period of wisdom and hope and prosperity unparalleled in the history of Israel. One child dies in justice, but another is given in mercy. Sin, even murder, is forgiven, and relationships are renewed. But evil is forthrightly condemned and put out in public to be dealt with. Then life goes on, redeemed, graced, and with renewed hope.

Murder, lust, and violence in kingdoms, governments, wars, and personal life are a reality, but they are not able to stop the presence of God from revealing itself or the Spirit of God from creating new possibilities. People who are totally human, weak, sinful, and even evil can still be beloved by God and forgiven. God remains faithful to all these people. Even out of sin comes grace. The pledge of God in the covenant to the nation will come true and be fulfilled, although not just as humans expect, plan, or devise. God rules history. The old adage, *Man proposes, God disposes,* is true. Bathsheba is now included in the nation. Her husband Uriah, who loved her, was faithful and would not be compromised. Bathsheba was married to a pagan who honored God in Israel and the ark of the covenant and paid for it with his death.

What is Bathsheba's connection to Mary? Perhaps it is in her children, one so intimate with violence that he is killed and another who becomes a sign of peace, wisdom, and the fulfillment of the promise of God's forgiveness in both justice and mercy. Bathsheba, like Mary, gives life, mourns the death of her son, and yet believes in life again.

And then Matthew brings us to Mary: "It was of her that Jesus who is called the Messiah was born" (Matthew 1:16). The genealogy is finished. History has moved to this moment—all things, all events, all people come together in this moment of grace, this relationship among Jesus, Mary, and Joseph.

Genealogies in Jewish history, as in our own, give patterns, define weaknesses, give connections between love, marriage, and blood ties, give authority and identity in the present and show forth hidden meanings that can be important now. So why these women? Why not Sarah, Rebecca, Rachel and Leah, Judith, or Deborah—women that many consider honorable, distinguished, worthy of memory? Why a woman who disguises herself as a prostitute and sleeps with her father-in-law and has twins? Why Tamar, who uses the law well beyond its customary limits to raise up children to her dead husband. Why Rahab, a Canaanite prostitute who becomes a spy and saves her whole clan and apparently marries and lives honorably in Israel? Why Ruth, a Moabite woman bound to her mother-in-law in a close relationship—two women who work with each other to get married, have children and grandchildren and stay together? Why Bathsheba, a woman taken in adultery, perhaps raped, and yet made queen and loved by David—a woman who loses both a husband and a child, yet has another husband and child that are renowned in Israel's history? They all use the law, break it, honor it, and see themselves under its weight and promise. Rahab and Ruth are converts. Tamar and Rahab both put their honor and integrity in jeopardy for what they want, and even Bathsheba is looked upon kindly as a beautiful woman who happens to be caught up in events that she cannot control or change.

It seems that Jesus' ancestors have not been uniformly neat, orderly, clean, honorable, or ordinary—like most people's ancestors. Jesus is born with the blood of these men and women in his veins. These women all fought for life, for children, for the continuation of hope, for generation, even if they did so in unorthodox ways. And they are all connected to Mary, because her own giving birth and the circumstances around the conception and bearing of Jesus are shady and shadowed and not normal. Jesus is a son of Abraham and David through Joseph, but he is also a son of Mary and many remarkable women who were feisty enough to make sure they and their children, even the unborn, would be a part of the promise. Mary, like many of these women, took risks. Tamar, Rahab, Ruth, Bathsheba, and Mary are memorable, worth wondering over, studying, and imitating. Mary is a new Tamar, a new Rahab, a new Ruth, a new Bathsheba, and a new woman in relationship to Joseph, a new and just man. Men and women become holy, become free, become something altogether new because of this child, this one child whom all the world and all history has awaited.

And us—who are we? Will we be remembered for this newness, this faithfulness, this courage, this passion and devotion to life and the future of generations, this fierce determination to be friends to one another and God? Will we be included in genealogies of disciples and believers that are passed on to our children and our grandchildren? These women give Israelite history and Jesus' ancestors flesh and blood, personality, and eccentricity—will we? Will we be remembered as having anything in common with Tamar, Rahab, Ruth, the wife of Uriah (Bathsheba), and Mary? Will stories be told of how we interrupted history and revealed something of God by our choices, decisions, and actions on behalf of life? Will people wonder about us and marvel at our compassion and love, our protection of the weak and poor, our care for widows and our friendship with outcasts, foreigners, and those unwed, pregnant, and ignored by others? Will we make the history of the children of God, the brothers and sisters of Jesus, worth reading and imitating?

No matter what is in our past—violence, murder, adultery, incest, prostitution, dishonesty, hypocrisy, loneliness, dislocation from place and community, abuse of power, deceitfulness, lack of faithfulness—it doesn't matter. All is forgiven. Justice is served. Hope is restored. Mercy and peace are given. God works with whatever! If God can bring forth Jesus, the sun of justice, the child of peace, the hope of the nations, the light of the world from this history, what does the Spirit and grace intend for us? This child born of Mary, befriended by Joseph and conceived by the Spirit of God that took Mary under its wings, changes everything, opens up doors and windows in a household, cleans out the attic and invites in anyone, blood kin, friend, sojourner, foreigner, stranger, even enemy, and calls them family, beloved of God. He tells them there is room for all, for anyone who decides to hear the word of the Lord, believe the stories, hope in the promise, and submit to the one who makes all the stories of God come true.

The next generations and genealogies are ours to write with the Spirit and to discover what God can do with us, human beings who are graced and birthed in water and in blood and commanded to go into the whole world and bring this kingdom of hope to our history. We are called to believe that anything is possible. The future does not depend on sin or evil or failure or the old rules and ways. Even now God is making a new thing. Even now God is writing a new destiny, because this child Jesus has saved his people from their sins. His name is Emmanuel, "God with us," and dreams do come true.

# 5

# THE CANAANITE WOMAN

A little more than halfway through Matthew's gospel there is a very strange story of an encounter between a Canaanite woman and Jesus. The story is also found in Mark 7:24-30 with some minor changes—there the woman is described not only as a Canaanite, but as a Syro-Phoenician, a Greek. In addition, Jesus is specifically in someone's house where he doesn't want to be recognized or seen. It is a remarkable story of a woman intent on having Jesus pay attention to her very personal and specific request to help her daughter, and yet it is remarkable not merely for the individuality of the encounter.

The story is set in the territory of Tyre and Sidon, the seacoast area north of Galilee (around Beirut in today's Lebanon). Both Jesus and the woman are outside of their native places, both looking for something, both in need, and both strangers. And they are strangers to one another as well—she a woman and he a man; she a Greek/Canaanite and he a Jew. They are different in race, nationality, gender, religion, and probably politics and economics as well. It is a meeting across cultures, across boundaries and borders, a meeting that is pivotal to Matthew's understanding of Jesus' journey and Jesus' awareness of who he is and what his mission to the Jewish people entails.

I've told this story and discussed it in a number of cross-cultural settings in the United States, Canada, and in England, and it provokes a wide variety of reactions and responses because of the nature of the conversation that develops between Jesus and the woman, who is not named. But let us let the story begin to speak for itself.

*Then Jesus left that place and withdrew to the district of Tyre and Sidon. It happened that a Canaanite woman living in that locality presented herself, crying out to him, "Lord, Son of David, have pity on me! My daughter is terribly troubled by*

*a demon." He gave her no word of response. His disciples came
up and began to entreat him, "Get rid of her. She keeps shouting after us." "My mission is only to the lost sheep of the
house of Israel," Jesus replied. She came forward then and did
him homage with the plea. "Help me, Lord!" But he answered,
"It is not right to take the food of sons and daughters and
throw it to the dogs." "Please, Lord," she insisted, "even the
dogs eat the leavings that fall from their masters' tables." Jesus
then said in reply, "Woman, you have great faith! Your wish
will come to pass." That very moment her daughter got better
(Matthew 15:21-28).*

The description is simple. The characters are clearly presented. Jesus is traveling with his disciples, though the disciples are more observers than participants here. They
certainly are not helpful to the woman! And the woman, who
just happens to be living in that locality now, has a daughter
who is terribly troubled by a demon.

Often when we read the scriptures we react and hear them
as individuals, personally and spiritually, especially if the
need or the style of the encounter touches us. We forget that
all the stories have historical backgrounds, theological ramifications, and sociological contexts. They include the realities
of prejudice, nationalism, religious bias, and the basic human
needs of sickness, death, exclusion, racism, and cultural envi-
ronments that we often subsume into our own present-day
realities. Thus we react out of our twentieth-century Western
culture, and our bias overlays our hearing of the scripture.

Another thing we need to remember is that the scriptures
deal with the two poles or extremes of prophecy and pity.
The first is the Word, pure and evocative, out of the mouth
of God in the tradition of prophets, singers of the psalms, and
poets. Prophecy lays down a foundational base of experience
and context and stands there and speaks, calling everyone —
not as individuals, but as the people of God — to repentance,
transformation, and faithfulness. The other end of the spectrum is pity — tender regard for the person, the one or the few
people caught not just in the glare of the Word of the prophet,
of God, but in the net and broken web of the community that

allows individuals to be excluded, isolated or rejected. What draws prophecy and pity together and integrates them is the person of Jesus, the human Son of God standing both as the Word from all eternity and the Word spoken here in this time and place with great care and specificity. It is Jesus' passion, for the Father, for obedience, for truth, and for sinners and the poor that pulls the two together and makes them whole, holy, and all of a piece. It is the meeting and being held in that passion, that person, that reveals to us the depth of the meaning of the Word proclaimed in our midst. The presence of the Spirit in Jesus and in all of us is what negotiates and translates the common ground between prophecy and pity. Presence, time shared and developed together, words savored and chewed are the bridge that connects the two senses of power in the Word: prophecy and pity. And the time spent in hearing and discovery as well as the time spent in putting into practice is the bridge that reveals and draws forth the well of understanding of any particular text or story.

The story of the Canaanite woman is one in which we need to look beyond our initial reactions. It is important that we not react within our limited social contexts to the very personal story of a woman approaching a man in a setting where neither one of them is entirely at home. She just happens to be living there and Jesus is resting (withdrawing) and visiting. But the truth of the story lies beyond the specific details. The truth is universal, cross-cultural, interracial, dialogical, and alive—it moves between the story, the context of the teller, and those who hear, including us. Like all the scripture stories, this encounter reveals to us deeper realities of who we are and how to live if we are believers, if we are truly human.

Many people feel that this story is one of those that needs to be sounded out in community, preferably in a community composed of those of different ages, men and women, of various cultures, and races, people with varying levels of education—the range of reactions, insights, and thoughts that this story provokes can best be digested and put into perspective in such a community. The story hits many nerves and sensitive areas as well as triggering emotions close to our own present and past experiences—far removed from the cultural,

religious and geographical (and thus racial) settings at the
time of the story.

Let us read the text again and let the Spirit seep through,
touching our feelings and guts. The way we hear the text is
personal. We want our equality and individuality recognized;
we want to be taken seriously, not lumped in a group, or
treated differently. What feelings does the story, taken as a
story, stir? Reactions usually center on Jesus: what he's doing
and why. This Jesus seems out of character, or perhaps is
testing her, or he's just downright rude, insensitive, and
harsh. Men and women react to this reading very differently,
though both are troubled by Jesus' seeming rudeness.

Taking Jesus' actions and words as human responses in this
situation because of who he is, where he is coming from, and
what he has on his mind opens up still more questions. It
would be easier if he "turned on" his God-side and related
to her (and so to us) as the teacher, the one separate from our
realities, all-sure of what his behavior is going to be in every
situation. We see that as Jesus' rightful place. But maybe it's
not where he was or where we are today—any of us. We're
not used to dealing with this kind of Jesus. Some people react
very strongly: "I don't like Jesus ... He's an elitist snob ...
He treats her like dirt ... It's totally unnecessary the way he
deals with her—as though she wasn't really a person worth
his time." But then someone invariably says: "But he's a Jew
and a man and she's a Canaanite and a woman. His response
isn't that different from the way many of us deal with people
of other cultures, races, and religions. Look at the way we
talk about Muslims, Iranians and Iraqis, and the way Jews
speak of Palestinians." But *Jesus* acting like that? Does Jesus
have prejudices, nationalistic tendencies, problems with those
who aren't Jews? Is Jesus that human? Does he have to deal
with those kinds of things, as we do? Was Jesus affected by
being born in a specific locality, time frame, history, and cultural background? Why not? He's human too, like us in all
things except sin.

After the initial reactions the questions of who, what,
when, and where help to broaden the base of our reflections.
What kind of Jesus is this? He seems impatient, annoyed at

being interrupted. He recognizes his mission—who he is—but not in relation to this woman. He sees himself as being sent only to the lost sheep of the house of Israel, not to Canaanites, Syro-Phoenicians, Greeks, whatever. She's a distraction or problem outside the realm of his teaching and preaching.

Jesus has withdrawn. Obviously he wants to pray, to be by himself, to rest, to get away from others. The last thing he wants is to be bothered by a stranger. He has left his own place and his own people, the Pharisees and Israel, because they are rejecting him. They don't want to hear his teaching, his prophecies, his preaching, his announcement of the reign of God in the world. Jesus has just had major confrontations with the Pharisees. He called them hypocrites and summoned the crowd and told them that their leaders are the blind trying to lead the blind (Matthew 15:1-14). Jesus is annoyed and frustrated with his own people, disappointed, and rejected, so he goes off alone, away from the center of Jewish learning, life, and prophecy, to look again at himself and his mission. All he wants is some breathing space, time apart, time to reflect and decide how to continue his mission in the face of rejection and misunderstanding by his own people. This is one more interruption. And his disciples are feeling the same way; the mission is not going the way they expected. They are not being accepted by the Jerusalem Pharisees and scribes. They are uncomfortable, unsure of themselves, and nervous. The last thing they want is to be noticed, singled out, accosted. Then this woman approaches them in public. Their response is to ignore her. They go to Jesus and say: Do something, get rid of her, she's making a spectacle of herself and us, she's shouting after us and others are beginning to take notice.

Jesus' needs are crucial too, just as crucial as the woman's. His disciples' wishes and fears and all those individual and differing needs are rubbing against each other like sandpaper. And what about the daughter who has a terrible demon plaguing her? The woman and the daughter have the need to live an ordinary life, without being tormented. A demon—it could be insanity, any kind of disease that comes and goes with fits, loss of control—is debilitating and humiliating for both of them. A mother and her child—there is no mention of father or other family.

What bothers us in this story? For one thing, Jesus doesn't respond to her right away. His pity is not immediately forthcoming. The woman pleads, crying out: "Lord, Son of David, have pity on me!"Our image or expectation of Jesus, of God, is that as soon as we cry out God is supposed to react instantaneously. The woman shouldn't have to wait or ask again or be ignored. Jesus is supposed to put aside his own thoughts, feelings, problems, and struggles to deal with hers, and do so immediately. That is the way Jesus is—not like us, humans who need time to shift focus, to redirect our feelings from our pressing problems and doubts and thoughts about who we are and what we are doing, especially in the presence of rejection and misunderstanding. It makes a big difference whether we hear this story from the point of view of the woman in need—or Jesus in need. They are both hurting, both looking for help, insight, and a way to survive in their worlds; no one else seems to care very much if either of them is taken care of adequately.

Jesus needs time, space, and prayer in order to grow, to discern, to change, to develop, and to come to a deeper and truer understanding of his identity, his mission, his calling, his way of obeying the will of God in his life. He is struggling with the sense of who he is: a prophet sent to the lost sheep of the house of Israel and the dawning of the difficult and painful realization that they do not want him, are not listening, and are beginning to reject and fight him and his message. His identity as a prophet, a preacher, and teacher, as Messiah, is at stake.

The woman too is desperate, alone with a daughter who suffers from a demon—a disease that isolates and makes people afraid and also causes others to assume they have sinned. Any kind of disease was seen as punishment from God on those who deserved it. She is doubly cast aside—as stranger and as mother of a daughter so afflicted. Both the woman and Jesus are cast aside, adrift in their lives, seeking and looking for hope, a future and some compassion.

There is much that bothers us in this story, and much that

calls us to conversion. We see a different image of Jesus and are forced to deal with it. Jesus and the woman both are intent, passionate, single-hearted, and devoted to what they are doing. Both of them have a sense of mission. Jesus sees himself as sent to the lost sheep of the house of Israel, and he anguishes over the lost sheep, his people's rejection of hope, his people's rejection of him as a prophet sent from the Father. The woman sees herself on a mission to Jesus on behalf of her daughter, to save her from ruin, from illness, and from being discarded by others. Both Jesus and the woman live on behalf of others — Jesus as prophet sent to a people and the woman as a person with blood ties and love who daily cares for someone in desperate need. They have much in common, these two unlikely people meeting on neutral territory — perhaps, as a young woman once speculated — sent to each other by the Spirit. One woman with a mother's love for her child and one prophet with God's love for all God's children embody a clash of justice and systems and philosophy and the need for personal daily responses. They are speaking different languages, using different vocabularies to express their needs.

Often people say that their clash is what is more worthy or less worthy of attention — two ends of a spectrum — worthy or unworthy. But a better way of looking at it is a priority of needs. Jesus has come to the lost sheep of the house of Israel, the bottom layer of a group — already a rather substantial group to take care of and call home, bring back to God. The woman is dealing with one child, a daughter in need, the lost sheep of "no house," even less important and more in need perhaps than the lost sheep of Israel, more forgotten than Israel's sinners. Jesus and the woman live in their own worlds, their own cultures, religions, day-to-day lives, and each world is small. That is immediately apparent when their worlds collide: the world of the Jewish prophet who is being rejected and the world of the single mother with a daughter who consumes her every moment and thought.

These worlds exist in our churches, parishes, communities, even families. The worlds of justice and of charity, as some would describe them. The world of organizing and the world of corporal works of mercy, the world of administration and legal work and the world of daily tending to the repetitious needs of care of the homeless, sick, old, very young, disabled, and others. Within the clash of priorities and vocabularies, people look for a common language, a common bond, and understanding in order to move beyond their specific focus and intent—for both worlds are important, both are part of awareness and life, both are part of spirituality. They affect our consciousness of our person and mission, our self-identity, and awareness of hands-on justice, care for the individual in front of us who desperately needs attention now and the continuing needs of the many that can be dealt with only systematically through organization and change of structures.

There are always needs that are greater than our individual ones. As Christians of one particular area we have needs of spirituality, of identity, of charity, justice, and compassion; yet we are Christians of the universal church as well, and that larger church has needs, massive needs related to health care, food, daily survival, persecution, devastating poverty, lack of education, pollution, declining resources, and lack of access to the dominant cultures that control the possibility of many peoples' future on the earth. Which needs take priority? How do we balance our needs as individuals and as church and as nation with others' needs as individuals and peoples? This story is about one such encounter.

There is still more to deal with. Even if such a conflict is taking place, what about Jesus' reply and the woman's humiliation in the interchange between them? It sounds heartless, demeaning, disgusting, especially to people who see insult in the conversation, not faith. Let's go back and see the way the story develops and what actions and gestures and other interchanges lead up to the specific closing dialogue.

First, the woman presents herself, crying out to Jesus, calling him Lord, Son of David. She acknowledges him for who he is, which is more than most of his own people do. She honors him, obviously aware of the Jewish religion and some of its beliefs. She presents herself to him as one would an offering, as one who is not worthy but is in need, as one who has no rights but is asking out of sheer necessity. She asks for pity. She is a beggar, with hand and heart out on her sleeve in public.

Jesus ignores her, gives her no individual response, does not engage her in conversation, acts as though she isn't really there. This is not so terrible really—how do we react to beggars on the street, people we do not know who present themselves in our path? Mostly we hope they will go away if we ignore them. After all, what are we expected to do? There is no bond of connection, no similarity between us (except their need and presence and our availability and our obvious capability to help). In this case the woman seems to know who he is. She states her need: "My daughter is terribly troubled by a demon" (Matthew 15:22). She asks for another, not for herself.

Then there is the interruption by the disciples. They do not respond to her either, and when they turn to Jesus, there is no encouragement on their part for Jesus to acknowledge her request. Their suggestion is: "Get rid of her. She keeps shouting after us" (Matthew 15:23). They view her presence as a problem; they do not wish to be caught up in something that has nothing to do with them (or Jesus).

Jesus, however, doesn't do what they suggest. Instead, he speaks to his disciples and to her only as a side listener who will pick up the message: "My mission is only to the lost sheep of the house of Israel" (Matthew 15:24). His mission is only— only!—to those in Israel, people of the covenant who are lost, sinners, broken-hearted, bent and bowed down as the prophets before him have indicated. This is his path, his way, his identity, his destiny. It is an explanation of who he is and what he does and why. It is a secondhand acknowledgment that the title she uses in addressing him is true: son of David's house, a specific people's hope and Messiah and healer, but not hers.

The woman hears and responds by coming forward and doing him homage. Her move is probably even more disconcerting to the disciples than her shouting. Homage is done in many ways in many cultures and gestures, but it is always humbling to the one giving homage and it always honors outwardly the one who is approached with reverence. She may bow down, or kneel, or bend over, or kiss his feet, his hand, the hem of his cloak. Whatever she does, it is a sign of great respect, of honor, of submission. She is a foreign woman approaching a Jewish man, humbly begging a favor she knows she has no right to. She sees Jesus more clearly than many of his own Jewish people, certainly more clearly than his disciples. And she prays again: "Help me, Lord!" (Matthew 15:25). She prays for his attention, his response, any response to her prayer, her desperate condition, her love for her child.

The dialogue begins in his answer to her. (Remember, she is doing homage — she is still on the ground, bent over, kneeling, whatever.) "It is not right to take the food of sons and daughters and throw it to the dogs" (Matthew 15:26). Jesus' words are hard to take and hard to understand for many reasons. We are not first-century Jews; we are of another time and place. Any reference to people as dogs is insulting and derogatory in our culture. It is an insult, a metaphor that sees others not as human beings, but animals as eating leftovers, garbage, being dirty, unkempt, and disgusting. Could Jesus be saying what many Jews (and many people of religion today) say, that she is a dog, not a Jew, not worthy of his attention, and not part of his mission? And even if he is, it is her reply that is startling and unbelievable for us: "Please, Lord, even the dogs eat the leavings that fall from their masters' tables" (Matthew 15:27). She acknowledges what belongs to whom, what she is and what she is not — she is *not* a Jew, *not* of the house of Israel, and so not of his original mission, not one of his first choices to approach and save. But she again puts herself, this time verbally as she has before physically, in the position of servant or slave. She calls him Lord, refers to him as master, and humbly says that she, like dogs at the table in the household, will gladly take the leftovers of his mission and power and identity as prophet and Lord and eat what the sons and daughters throw away and do not eat at the table. She will take from him what his own will not.

In her need, her love for another, she encounters Jesus as Lord. Her faith and hope are born of the Spirit through her daughter's illness and their rejection. Jesus is astounded at her faith, her acknowledgement of him and who he is—as an outsider, a Canaanite, a Greek, a Syro-Phoenician, not a Jew, not of the lost sheep, just a woman who loves her child, a human being in need, someone willing to humble herself to beg for another's healing and hope. She is like him, and Jesus not only responds to her, but he praises her: "Woman, you have great faith!" (Matthew 15:28). He speaks directly to her and gives her her wish—her daughter's health and hope for a future together. It is in that moment that the woman puts the words and the hope and the belief into practice. She leaves him and goes to find her daughter better. The word must have spread about the encounter and the outcome when she returned home to her child. The woman, as he calls her, a term of honor and respect, has great faith, more than his own people and his own disciples. He is accepted, honored, acknowledged, and revealed as Lord, as Son of David, sent to the lost sheep of the house of Israel and now to anyone who approaches him in hope, in need, and in faith, to anyone who humbles himself or herself before him and acknowledges his mission.

Jesus immediately moves on along the sea of Galilee, and large crowds of people come to him. He goes up the mountainside, and they come to him. He heals many, and there is great astonishment as they behold what is happening, what he is doing, and they glorify the God of Israel. Then Jesus' heart is moved to pity by the crowds, and he feeds them— four thousand, not counting the women and children!

Then Jesus moves on to the district of Magadan. He moves on, not just from that place, but from the world he thought he came for and belonged to. He moves from a limited understanding of himself as the prophet and teacher only to the lost sheep of the house of Israel. Now his mission is to the world—all the peoples of the earth and all the lost children of God. This moving on will eventually extend to the whole world, for Matthew's gospel ends with the command to his disciples to "go ... and make disciples of all nations," and with his promise that he will be with them in the world, until the end of time, with all peoples, in all places with all who acknowledge him as Lord and savior. His mission is to all sinners, all lost sheep, all children of God.

The Syro-Phoenician woman persists; she stays with the Word of God, the presence of Jesus, in her need and desire, and she is given what she needs and wants and more! She is given honor by Jesus, praise and acceptance into his company, his house, and his community, as well as a life of hope and a future for herself and her daughter. And Jesus is given an insight into himself, an extension of his mission and identity, a connection to another world, to seeing himself not only sent to the lost sheep of the house of Israel, but to all and everyone who will listen and honor his message and his God, to anyone who cares for all the children of earth, all nations and races and religions and cultures. There is room in the kingdom for all. That moment was hope for Jesus as well as for mother and daughter.

The disciples witness this encounter, though nothing is expressed about their reaction or whether they understand what is happening between Jesus and this unknown mother. Jesus knows, but the woman probably does not realize that she has altered Jesus' course and life in that moment. In her need and passion and love Jesus learns universal love and service and extends his mission past his own people, his own religion, and his own nation. From here on, in Matthew's gospel, Jesus acts from this new vantage point, this new perspective and new identity. The gospel is for *all* peoples, first to the lost sheep of the house of Israel, but then just as graciously and generously and mercifully to all who believe and obey.

Many people still have difficulty believing that Jesus would speak to her so, as a Jew, culturally, and so seemingly prejudiced. There are other explanations. Some scholars and scripture exegetes say that Jesus was using language that was couched in images and metaphors, a style of dialogue that wasn't insulting but playful or descriptive of his reluctance to move toward an outsider. And she hears the imagery and plays along with it, accepting Jesus on his terms, playing back with him. Whatever the explanation, the encounter calls us, as individuals and as community of Jesus, to a deeper belief and a change of heart and attitude.

Jesus is a Jew, a member of the chosen people—and she was not chosen. God gave choice portions to the chosen people, and she was not chosen first. We consider ourselves as the chosen people of God, and we have been given the choice portions. As residents of the First World, using the bulk of the world's resources, we are the ones at the table and everyone else is under the table, as dogs, feeding on the leftovers that we throw their way. The conversation between Jesus and this woman reveals on a deeper level the realities of politics, economics, religion, racism, and nationalism that existed then and exist now. The brief encounter of these two human beings reveals to us today what is happening, what shouldn't be happening, and what could be happening. The woman and Jesus find a way to have both their individual needs met on an immediate basis. Further, Jesus leaves changed, as radically changed as the daughter who gets better. The Spirit worked in and through both Jesus and the woman to change them, move them, and so move all of us who have ears to hear the message in what is transpiring between them.

We members of the First World *do* have the choice portions, and everyone else operates as the dogs under our table; too often we don't even give the leftovers to the others begging from us. Jesus tells it like it is, and the woman knows and accepts and understands. The two of them become one in the Spirit. We think that she is humiliated, and that Jesus humiliates her further, but a woman from Mexico once said in a group: "She's already down. She knows it, and she knows what she needs, and she learns Jesus' language, and they both are given what they need from the lack in the other." Jesus needed her need, and she needed Jesus' rejection and searching, and they both are made whole. She uses another culture, language, symbols, relationships, ways of viewing the world and incorporates them into her world, and in the struggle they both discover a way into the future.

· This story has massive consequences for our prayer, ministry, especially cross-cultural ministry, encounters with those who are not members of our religious groups. It profoundly influences our imaging of Jesus as God and how God works in the world, prophetically and with pity, in justice and mercy, individually and collectively. It says the best way to begin is prayer—begging, humbling ourselves before another person (culture, community) and seeing from that vantage point, from below, as servant, as one who learns, as one who comes not with the answers or the insights but in need, lacking, open, and receptive. It says we need to learn to use another's language, culture, gestures, expressions, and style for dialogue in respect and humility. It says that the strongest authority and power is begging and pleading on behalf of others, not for ourselves, and that kind of relationship allows us to humble ourselves. It says we must believe in the other's word (after all, the woman goes off with just Jesus' word, no tangible experience, to find that her daughter got better in that moment). That moment, that encounter, has ripple effects beyond our choices, words, and experiences, effects on those we love, are bonded to, live with in community, and the larger crowds that come to hear of it. Both Jesus and the woman go their own way. Yet each goes the way—the way to Jerusalem and the cross and into the world for Jesus, the way of Jesus in the woman and her daughter's life. Everyone changes after an encounter with the Word in the community or the Word in the life of two people.

Any encounter or understanding of the Word changes our way of seeing God, of relating to God and others. Our image of God must keep growing, expanding, and going deeper, becoming more inclusive of others, especially those we do not esteem, acknowledge, or even notice as worthy of our engagement. They perhaps know or have access to seeing us in a way that we need and are searching for. The answers to our doubts, questions, and hopes lie in others' beliefs, needs, and searching, very rarely in ourselves. A young man suggested that the story says that God loves us especially when we persist, argue, and humble ourselves to keep the conversation going, especially when God is in another person who is not like us. If that is true, differences are not to be seen as problems in a community or city but as open doorways to the presence of God that reveals and leads us to a more fruitful, creative, healing understanding on both sides.

All human beings experience the fruits of any two people

meeting in the Word. And the leftovers, the scraps that are thrown to the dogs under the table, the refuse of others in relation to God — they are more than enough to live on. God's scraps are food and hope, bread and justice, mercy and healing. Are we sharing the food on the table, or are we hoarding more than we need, keeping others from what they need desperately — food, economics, resources, faith, prayer, reconciliation, healing, and the corporal and spiritual works of mercy? Do we, like the woman, take anything God gives, knowing the power of even what is thrown to the dogs? Do we live gladly on whatever God gives to us?

This is Matthew's gospel, a word of hope to Jewish people who have become Christians and have been rejected from the Jewish community and daily life. This is a story of hope, of being drawn in after rejection, of extension into the larger world, of a broader vision and promise, of a belief and a message for all, of a new identity not just for Jesus, but for Matthew's community and for us, as the universal church. We all belong, we all need one another, we must learn one anothers' cultures, languages, gifts of race and nation, place and face. It is in the other that our needs are met and our journeys continued; in us others find hope, solace, and their needs answered. We are together on the way to the cross and resurrection, and there is room, in fact special places, for those not previously considered welcome or of value and worth. We must all change, accommodate, learn another's tongue, and accept that underneath we are all human beings, all children of God. If we are given choice portions at the table, we must be very careful not to take that for granted and waste it or hoard it. We must live openly, respectful of differences and remember that the Spirit is the sacrament let loose in the world and is everywhere trying to approach us in creative and wondrous ways, and that all serves God's reign and the coming of the presence of justice, mercy, and hope in our midst. Just because we don't see how someone fits, does not mean that the person is to be ignored or forgotten or excluded — maybe we need him or her to reveal the way of God to us in this moment. If Jesus can be instructed and comforted by an unknown stranger who approaches him in need, then who may serve to teach us?

The basis of this story, and of all the gospel, is how to alleviate human misery — the misery of the ones close to us and the misery of all the lost children of God. It is the same story, expanding and shrinking in our sight and presence; it asks us to look at justice and mercy, prophecy and pity in our lives and see how we weave together politics, race, nationalism, theology, and our personal life in this history and place where the Spirit still lies hidden, waiting to be revealed in every meeting, every need, especially whenever two or three are gathered in the name of the Lord, the name of the Trinity, the name of God, no matter what name we call God by in our tradition, culture, or awareness.

What does the story tell us to start looking at politically, religiously, economically, racially? We must begin by looking at our language. We speak two or three or more languages all the time. We have the language of our birth and sometimes second languages learned in school or out of necessity or intent. We have the language of our prayer and spirituality and devotion, and sometimes another theological language from academics and study or position. We have the language of our jobs and professions, and we have political language and the language of our families. There are many other languages: psychological languages, self-help languages, the language of poetry and song, the languages of economics, law, nationalities, and the languages of slang particular to our small groups, geographically, ethnically, and culturally. We forget that those languages can confine, confuse, and blur communication as well as offer us possibilities for encounter and understanding of others. We need to ask if our languages are touching or missing the languages of others — evangelizing, praying, communicating, asking questions, putting forth agenda. We must become translators and help people understand each other.

In this story the woman is desperate about her child — what does she care about theological language? Just because a particular way of speaking helps us to express ourselves and our level of understanding or impression of God and life, it does not necessarily help another, especially if his or her needs are different from ours. To demand, to impose, arbitrarily to change languages for our own usefulness, sense of identity, and power, or to refuse to learn another's language is to block the Spirit, to hinder the possibility of a future, certainly between peoples, but also between individuals, sometimes those in desperate need.

Language must serve human beings in their particular circumstances, not just *our* particular insights and *our* position at the moment. Our attitude toward another—any other—must be one of respect, honor, dignity, and care, even as we struggle to communicate and meet one another's needs, knowingly or unknowingly. Those of us with power must learn how to use that power in meeting the human needs of others who call us forth and demand that our power be used on their behalf, not always as we intend or want or see our role. Those in need must continually and steadfastly push those with power, authority, and the ability to change situations to move, to act on their behalf, and both must change, be converted in the presence of the other and the Word of God. No one escapes conversion.

In the story Jesus' change will turn him in the direction of the cross. The woman's change will also affect her life forever; she has encountered Jesus, and there is now a relationship between them. The disciples will have to learn that Jesus' identity and ministry will affect them drastically, leading to life-and-death situations in their future. If we truly wish to serve, to minister to others, we must honor and know and listen to their languages carefully. We cannot assume they understand ours or that ours better approaches meaning or communication. This is especially important for ministers in the church and community who bring with them languages of liturgy, of theology, of methodology, of ministry, of pedagogy, of tradition—languages that are not necessarily the common languages of those they come to serve. The community cannot be expected to keep up with all the new genres, expressions, spiritualities, and developments in theology (and their jargon). The community's languages of prayer, of devotion, of daily life, and of need must be respected, heard, and translated for others. At heart, it begins with us, as individuals and communities. Are we willing to learn another's language—those on our borders, those on the next street, those who pray next to us in church but speak another tongue? A person's language reveals his or her place in the world, not from our vantage point but the person's. The Spirit works most often in ordinary human discourse, not in specific vocabularies or professional languages of power or education or the dominant culture.

There is also language that is nonverbal. There is presence and also the avoiding of certain people's presence. There is dealing with a personal need as opposed to fixing structures and policies. In this story Jesus changes his identity and policy and mission in attending to the immediate presence and need of a woman who will not be ignored. And the woman approaches Jesus, does homage, puts herself in a different position in relation to him. All these gestures and ways of being with and before another speak, often more than the words themselves. She humbles herself, worships, acknowledges, listens attentively to any words that Jesus says, whether directed to her or others, and responds. My grandmother used to say that "position in life is everything." She meant many things by that phrase—the way we are in relation to others, the way we present ourselves, and where things happen. The place is part of the relationship. What happens in this story has power because both Jesus and the woman are out of their usual spaces and places, displaced, visiting, withdrawing. Moments of spirituality, of ministry, and of insight happen as the Spirit wills, often in unlikely, out of the ordinary places with people we do not usually deal with. The result can be a change in our personal agenda and identity; it can have long-term consequences for what we do and how we do it. The individual must be remembered and related to always—doing so corrects policy, structures, institutions, and injustice. It also sensitizes those doing justice, probing and analyzing the structural bases and keeps them connected to daily reality.

In a way this story is really about the daughter, the child, the one not present, the dog under the table—not because of anything Jesus says, or even the Jewish beliefs and practices and philosophy, but because of the behavior and the injustice and ignorance of others, Jew and Gentile alike. She is terribly tormented, suffering. She has no life, no connections, no future, and no hope in her culture, her village, her home. What transpires between Jesus and her mother changes her life and others forever. Whatever is of the Spirit affects us individually and in our dealings with another; it brings hope and alleviates the sufferings and misery of the many who live like dogs. Whatever happens between us and God and in our self-awareness, or between us and others, must bring compassion and change the situation of those who only know life as rejected, lost, alienated, and forgotten. If whatever happens in our spiritual lives individually and in community does not have bearing on those who are not counted, then it is not of the Spirit, not of true religion, not pure and single-hearted devotion to the will of God, which wills life, hope, dignity, and abundance for all.

Jesus changed the position of the woman who approached him and her daughter's position in the community, and with that he discovers how to change the dream, the vision, and the mission of the larger group, the world he is now sent into as prophet and redeemer. The story ends with the comment that from that moment on the child got better. In that moment Jesus shifted places with that child. He embraced her not from a distance, but intimately, and aligned himself with her, the absent daughter, the child plagued by a demon and cast off from society and hope, and he stayed with her. Indeed, he stays with her and all those in that position, dying with them on the cross, buried in a borrowed grave, rejected still by his own, and betrayed and abandoned by his disciples and friends. The woman bends and does him homage, and Jesus responds by bending before us, all of us, and being willing to share the position of those under the table with the dogs, those dying on a garbage dump outside the city, those lower than even the dogs. Jesus shares the woman's undying love for her child, and in Jesus it is undying love for all of us, the children of God, who are lost without him.

This is a story about seeing and knowing and separating

out our personal and individual needs, thoughts, feelings, identities, and memories from the very real and larger needs of the world. It is about learning how to balance the two and letting both prophecy and pity meet in our presence with others. We learn to recognize prophecy and pity in the presence of others, but especially others who are different, more vulnerable, those who come as intrusions with poor timing and persistent demands, those who are not the ones we are used to dealing with, want to deal with, or see as ours.

Another disconcerting revelation of this gospel is how to approach power. The woman does what is needed, what has to be done to get her child taken care of. Most of us will not do what is needed. We will only go so far, not past any point or position that humbles us, puts us at a disadvantage, or aligns us with someone lower. We try to keep our vantage points, our positions of privilege, our places of power rather than taking the option for the poor, which is the fundamental imperative of the gospel, becoming poor in spirit or fact, practicing the virtue of poverty, and making ourselves more lowly for the sake of others in the kingdom. We do not have the love, the connection, or the single-hearted desire of the woman that is the edge of faith and the beginning of a new relationship with Jesus and an introduction to the way of the cross. She is willing to beg in public, to change languages, to do him homage, to be looked down upon by strangers (the disciples even), and to humiliate herself if that will get her what she desperately needs for a life. If she can do this, why can't we? We need her passion, which is the love and passion of God. We need to learn to humiliate ourselves before power or authority in order to change the reality of those who are humiliated all the time.

Someone once said that shaming people into goodness is not the best way, but it is one way. What would it mean to shame our governments into providing the basic necessities of life for the majority of the world's population, which is terribly tormented by the lack of them now? What would it mean to shame our churches into caring for the homeless, unemployed, single parents, and deprived families in our parishes? What would it mean to shame our prayer and scripture

groups and parish committees into doing the corporal works
of mercy? What would it mean to shame our religious communities into caring and providing for the real needs of the
church in service as expressions of the vows of poverty and
obedience rather than as individual jobs and professional
bases of power in the structure? These questions are about
power, about authority, about how we serve others' needs,
look to our own, and think about changing structures in the
church and in the world. The woman calls forth Jesus' power
and extends it, and in so doing changes him forever. She is a
gift to him, a minister to him. She empowers him, enables
him, and reveals him to himself at least as much if not more
than what he does for her and her child in that moment. The
power she unleashes in him spreads out into other districts,
other religions, and makes people who are not Jews praise
the God of Israel — remarkable indeed.

Jesus learns in his "withdrawing" that we can never get
away from who and what we are. It stays with us. We are
children of God, commissioned and sent to others, whether
we are comfortable with who we think we are and what and
how we are doing it or not. Who others think we are, in the
context of the Spirit, is just as crucial, if not more so. The
Spirit calls us forth through others — their needs, prayers,
homage, relationships, interruptions. That tension and uneas-
iness is where the Spirit moves and operates and expresses
itself, where it uses power to make holy and undo whatever
destroys life. This story sheds light on the meaning of prayer,
ministry, justice and compassion, worship, healing and aiding
others in distress, and our identity as believers, as prophets,
as servants. They are all of a piece. And worship, conversion,
ministry, our identities are found in basic human experiences,
in relationships, in family, in suffering and addictions, in
rejection, and in outside forces that suddenly infringe on us
because of circumstances and the choices of others. The Spirit
is present everywhere and in everyone, lurking, ready to
pounce, playing off everyone's sensitivities and needs. The
depth of our faith, the quality of our spirituality is in the
seeing, the discovering, the being taken advantage of, the
letting go of our previous assumptions and thoughts, agenda

and consciousness, images of God, and possibilities. God is in all the details, all the specifics, all the stories, all the places, all the experiences, especially in the ones we prefer to withdraw from. Through another we can convert, save, heal, and bring life if we have ears to hear and eyes to see and a heart that is open to the God who cares about Greeks, Syro-Phoenicians, Jews, Gentiles, Christians, Muslims, Buddhists, Native Americans, those terribly troubled and rejected by society, plagued by demons, and lost to any house.

Jesus learns in an instant and reorders his whole life. The disciples take a good deal longer to see what has happened in their midst and to realize that their way has just been altered drastically, that the road is much wider and the travelers more numerous than before. Despite their encounters with Jesus, time and time again, they took the choice portions and privileged encounters many times before they came to understand what the woman recognized in her poverty and need and unbounded love for her daughter. There are no limits to God and the way God loves and intervenes in the world except the limits we put on one another and so on the Spirit's ways among us. Humility brings forth the humble God, who is willing even to become human, live and die among us, share the rejection and discouragement of others, and accept the cross to save us. We, the disciples of this teacher Jesus, can learn much from the Canaanite woman, who taught him such largesse and generosity and wideness in his mercy and mission.

To call Jesus Lord is to respond to a place beyond borders and boundaries in this world, to that place called the kingdom of justice and mercy, the reign of God, the place of peace, the promise of hope. It is to obey any authority that is based on such unconditional love, responding to any expression of the Spirit wherever it is loose in the world. This kind of liberation and freedom and life transcends any local particularities, regional or personal histories, and existing structures, cultures, or dominant races and institutions. We are all one already in the life and death and resurrection of Jesus — our lives and spiritual journeys keep trying to remind us of that larger universal reality. We are one in the Lord, we live in communion as the children of God, and all peoples must share in the justice and hope of those to whom the choice portions are given. As long as there are dogs under the table — masses of people in misery, children who suffer terribly from demons, and people rejected by society and church—that is where Jesus is found. Misery and divisions are not compatible with the faith of Christians. They are not acceptable or justifiable or to be tolerated. The Lord calls all of us humbly to grow in awareness of God's unconditional love lavished on us and to share that love in all the ways the Spirit draws forth from us so that others may get better from the moment we encounter Jesus in the word and thereafter.

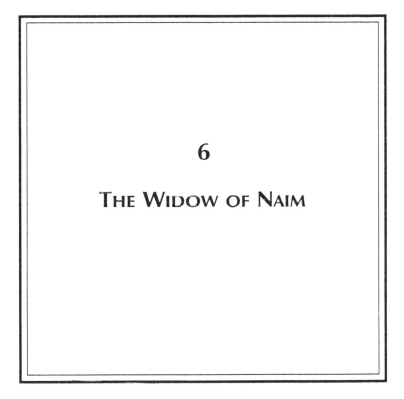

# 6

# THE WIDOW OF NAIM

I t seems that Jesus has a special fondness for widows, perhaps because his mother was one for most of her life. When he does something remarkable or finds something remarkable in the community, it is often connected to a widow. Widows are part of the group in the Jewish tradition that is known as the *anawim*—the poor ones of Yahweh. They are outcasts, fringe folk, people not seen as necessary to the community, problems to society, among those not counted. No one would choose to be part of this group, which is usually seen as suffering, alone, and without power. Yet this group is the criterion in the Jewish community for faithfulness. The way widows are treated, included, attended to, loved, and honored (or not!) reveals the level and depth of integrity and faithfulness to the covenant in the community of Yahweh's people. Whenever they are not cared for, not treated with dignity, not drawn into the life and worship of the community, a prophet is sent to defend them, to remind the community of its responsibilities and what will happen if it doesn't change its behaviors and attitudes. A prophet speaks on behalf of those who have no voice; a prophet is a reminder that God is on the side of those no one listens to, takes seriously, or worse, treats unjustly. And if these people are being treated unjustly by those who claim to be religious, righteous, or part of a group that claims to belong to God, then the prophet will stop at nothing to defend the honor of God and so care for the poor.

In some symbolic way, the honor of God is the care of the poor. For instance, in Mark's gospel a rich young man comes to Jesus wanting eternal life. He obeys the commandments, and Jesus looks at him with love, inviting him into his group of disciples, inviting him into a closer intimacy with Jesus. He tells the young man: to go sell what he has and give it to the poor, thus laying up treasure in heaven, then come follow

Jesus. We know from this story that our treasure in heaven is what we have done for the poor.

In the Jewish tradition the poor, the *anawim*, are the privileged presence, where the people of God practice their obedience to the covenant and reveal to the nations the presence of God in their midst. The poor are also a reminder of their former position as slaves in Egypt, which is never to happen to anyone in their community because of their behavior toward one another. They were rescued from oppression and forced labor and lack of human dignity and offered hope for the future and simple human life with gracefulness. They are never to become like their oppressors and allow anyone in their community to suffer so needlessly. To do so would be an insult to their God, who heard their cry and came to save them. And so, widows are usually the first mentioned in the listing of the *anawim*, along with orphans—women without protection in society and children without rights and recourse.

This story is about a woman, a widow from the town of Naim, whom Jesus meets on his way through town. It is also about her child and the people of the town, many of them her friends and neighbors, as well as Jesus' disciples.

*Soon afterward he went to a town called Naim, and his disciples and a large crowd accompanied him. As he approached the gate of the town a dead man was being carried out, the only son of a widowed mother. A considerable crowd of townsfolk were with her. The Lord was moved to pity upon seeing her and said to her, "Do not cry." Then he stepped forward and touched the litter; at this, the bearers halted. He said, "Young man, I bid you get up." The dead man sat up and began to speak. Then Jesus gave him back to his mother. Fear seized them all and they began to praise God. "A great prophet has risen among us," they said; and "God has visited his people." This was the report that spread about him throughout Judea and the surrounding country (Luke 7:11-17).*

When this story is proclaimed in a group, it inspires a wide range of emotions and feelings—joy, delight, exaltation, wonder, surprise, hope, enthusiasm, belief, even disbelief and doubt. How could there be people who didn't believe in someone who raised someone from the dead? But hardly anyone feels the emotion of the people present at the experience—fear. The people of Naim felt awe and reverence, because this phenomenon is part of their religious tradition. Their natural response to being in the presence of God, or God's emissary, prophet, or messenger is to praise God. If this action is possible, then it is connected to power, to God, and to the word of the prophet in their midst.

These people of Naim, of Israel, are religious people, steeped in their stories and traditions. Miracles (marvelous to behold) are manifestations of the presence of God among them, trying to get their attention, teach, proclaim and return them to the worship of God and practice of their religion. They are reminders of their place before God as one of great gratitude and indebtedness because of what God has done for them as a people in their history. They recall the Exodus, and Mount Sinai, and the promised land that they now live in as God's people, oppressed and Roman occupied territory, but the promised land nonetheless. They undoubtedly recall the story of Elijah and the widow:

*Elijah the Tishbite, from Tishbe in Gilead, said to [King] Ahab: "As the LORD, the God of Israel, lives, whom I serve, during these years there shall be no dew or rain except at my word." The LORD then said to Elijah: "Leave here, go east and hide in the Wadi Cherith, east of the Jordan. You shall drink of the stream, and I have commanded ravens to feed you there." So he left and did as the LORD had commanded. He went and remained by the Wadi Cherith, east of the Jordan. Ravens brought him bread and meat in the morning, and bread and meat in the evening, and he drank from the stream.*

*After some time, however, the brook ran dry, because no rain had fallen in the land. So the LORD said to him, "Move on to Zarephath of Sidon and stay there. I have designated a widow there to provide for you." He left and went to Zarephath. As he arrived at the entrance of the city, a widow was gathering sticks there; he called out to her, "Please bring me a small cupful of water to drink." She left to get it, and he called out after her, "Please bring along a bit of bread." "As the LORD your God lives," she answered, "I have nothing baked; there is only a handful of flour in my jar and a little oil in my jug. Just now I was collecting a couple of sticks, to go in and prepare something for myself and my son; when we have eaten it, we shall die." "Do not be afraid," Elijah said to her. "Go and do as you propose. But first make me a little cake and bring it to me. Then you can prepare something for yourself and your son. For the LORD, the God of Israel, says, 'The jar of flour shall not go empty, nor the jug of oil run dry, until the day when the LORD sends rains upon the earth.' " She left and did as Elijah had said. She was able to eat for a year, and he and her son as well; the jar of flour did not go empty, nor the jug of oil run dry, as the LORD had foretold through Elijah (1 Kings 17:1-16).*

Reactions to this story fall into three categories. The first is amazement that the widow obeys a total stranger, even referring to Elijah's God, not her own. She is destitute, alone with a child, and getting ready to prepare her last meal, and yet she obeys—first to get water, then to use the last of her oil and flour to make a cake for a stranger at the entrance to the city. Did she know who Elijah was? Or was she obeying hospitality laws and customs that mandated welcome for the stranger? In Jewish society even beggars were expected to give to others who begged from them, who were in even worse conditions. As an outsider—a foreigner and stranger in the city—Elijah was in that group of *anawim*, as was she, a widow, and her son. Her kindness, courtesy, and obedience, is rewarded with ongoing life and sustaining food until the rain comes.

The second type of response focuses on the way God takes care of the prophet—telling him to hide, where to go, and giving specifics on the Wadi water and the ravens who will feed him; then the instructions to go to another place, a specific town, Zarephath of Sidon, and that God has designated a widow there to provide for the prophet. (Of course, the widow doesn't know that she has been singled out by God to provide for the prophet's needs, though she obeys just like the ravens and the prophet!) It seems that prophets hide out in deserted places, with ravens and the poor and widows — God's obedient friends.

The third reaction questions why there is no rain for seven years? The answer entails backtracking to read the description of Ahab's reign in Israel. Ahab married Jezebel and worshiped Baal, a pagan god. Thus he angered God. In this time of unfaithfulness and disobedience to the covenant a prophet arose, the strongest and most wild of the prophets. Elijah is the forerunner of John the Baptist, the one who goes before the face of the Lord to prepare his way. There is no rain because there is no true worship. This is the background for the story of Elijah and the widow. It is a story of kindness, of obedience, of relationship, of need, and of honor among outsiders.

*Some time later the son of the mistress of the house fell sick, and his sickness grew more severe until he stopped breathing. So she said to Elijah. "Why have you done this to me, O man of God? Have you come to me to call attention to my guilt and to kill my son?" "Give me your son," Elijah said to her. Taking him from her lap, he carried him to the upper room where he was staying, and laid him on his own bed. He called out to the LORD: "O LORD, my God, will you afflict even the widow with whom I am staying by killing her son?" Then he stretched himself out upon the child three times and called out to the LORD: "O LORD, my God, let the life breath return to the body of this child." The LORD heard the prayer of Elijah; the life breath returned to the child's body and he revived. Taking the child, Elijah brought him down into the house from the upper room and gave him to his mother. "See!" Elijah said to her, "your son is alive." "Now indeed I know that you are a man of God," the woman replied to Elijah. "The word of the LORD comes truly from your mouth" (1 Kings 17:17-24).*

This is a most remarkable story, incredible, especially if it's true! It is definitely hard to believe, hard to take, hard to incorporate into our life in the twentieth century. These ways of God dealing with the people through a prophet and dealing with individuals who befriend the prophet are full of power and small details of intimacy, ordinariness, and at the same time, full of words of truth and revelation—for the widow and the prophet, and also for us.

The widow's child weakens and dies. The widow turns to Elijah, whom she calls a man of God, and questions him in her grief: Has this happened to me because of my guilt? It was the common understanding among ancient peoples that disaster, death, and destruction happened because of a person's behavior, or sin. The widow is reacting as many of us still do today—taking very personally what happens to another. She fears her son's death is connected to something she has done or failed to do. She fears a deity who deals with everything tit for tat, down to the last little jot and dotting of letters. Nothing escapes such a God.

But Elijah sees things differently. Elijah sees the widow and her son as part of the people being punished for the king's unfaithfulness and the state of the land and its people in its sin. And Elijah reminds the Lord not only of her obedience and care in feeding him, but that he is sheltered in her house and has his own room—she has been generous to him. She is not like the people. She practices and obeys the covenant injunctions in dealing with strangers and foreigners, let alone the other daily laws. The prophet gently reminds God of who she is, a widow without power, yet kind and generous. And then he prays, very physically, lying on top of the child's body, in words about breath. The image arises of the prophet lying on top of the child's corpse and breathing his own breath into the mouth of the child—sharing life and breath with the dead child. We are told that God hears Elijah's prayer, God revives the child. Elijah picks up the child and brings him back downstairs and gives him back to his mother. Earlier he had taken the child from her lap; now he gives him back. This child is her life as well, her future, the one who will take care of her in her old age, since she has no husband, no ties to the community that are bound in blood. Without her child she could die or be put outside the confines of the town to beg. The child is her hope for daily life. To save the child's life is to save hers as well.

Elijah is grateful to the widow and prays on her behalf to God; God honors his gratitude by returning the favor of life to the widow and her son. Life keeps changing hands, being passed around from God to raven, to prophet, from widow to prophet, from prophet to child and widow. But her response is not what we might expect. Instead of thanks, she acknowledges who Elijah is, a prophet. She says that the word of the Lord truly comes from his mouth. The word of the Lord is thus intimately connected to the power of life and death and to an intimate relationship with God that is essentially a relationship on behalf of the life and death of the people. The widow now recognizes and proclaims the reliability of Elijah's word—his call and vocation.

It is after this experience, long afterward, we're told, in the third year of the drought, that Elijah leaves the widow's house and goes to the king to provoke him and his court prophets. After the ritual encounter he seizes them all and slits their throats and then heads off into the mountains of Carmel to hide from Jezebel's wrath and to find God in the gentle breeze and stillness of the cave. Elijah, called "the disturber of Israel" by King Ahab, lives on a seesaw between raging passion and violence and gentle tenderness and prayer.

This story of the prophet Elijah, the one who is recognized publicly as having the word of the Lord in his mouth, the one who deals with life and death in his own breath and prayer and body, the one who lives on the kindness of the poor and ravens and widows and who knows the life of the fringe on the outside of society—this story of Elijah is the memory, the echo of Jesus, the prophet who raises from the dead the only son of the widow of Naim. The people of Naim recognize the word of God in the mouth of Jesus—truly.

Sometimes people's initial reaction to this story of Jesus and the widow's son is stunned silence. They start thinking of people facing death and the ramifications it has on families, friends, care-givers. It makes them think of all the prayers they say to save people from dying and their constant wondering if their prayers are heard and if they make any difference. But mostly they don't expect the person to get better, especially in the case of incurable diseases—they have great hopes and no expectations. But this is a story about someone who is already dead—the people are on their way to bury him!

Sometimes I ask people how they would react if they read this story in a newspaper or heard about it on a news report. The closing line of the account is, after all, just that—"This was the report that spread about him throughout Judea and the surrounding country" (Luke 7:17). The scene is a crowd of people surrounding a woman, obviously well known, and the funeral cortege of her son, her only son—and she is a widow. They are at the gate of the city, heading out to the burial grounds, and they meet another crowd, this one surrounding an itinerant preacher and his disciples heading into the city. Jesus is moved to pity upon seeing her in her distress; the first thing he says is, "Do not cry." Then he touches the bier, and the bearers halt. Jesus tells the dead son: "Young man, I bid you get up." And he does! Then Jesus gives him back to his mother.

Think about the newspapers and tabloids picking it up—the reactions. They would send out physicians to determine if the man really had been dead (reports would be conflicting); have interviews with the widow, the young man, all available townspeople, especially the bearers; exploit this sensational story for all it's worth. And if you were there—what effect would it have on you? Invariably someone points out that it would be terribly disruptive. The people know their role at a funeral. They are all prepared to have a dinner and reception afterwards. They know exactly what will happen. Then their crowd meets another. And soon, the dead son sits up and starts talking! Everybody's stomach is churning, hackles rise on the back of their neck. First they were watching the dead child, then the focus shifted to Jesus, then Jesus pushes the focus back to the child and the widow. Now fear seizes them all—this man has the power over death. That means he has power over life as well. Who is he? What is he? Where does his power come from? Everything is changed radically, drastically. Nothing will ever be the same again. The laws of nature no longer hold. What is sure? What can be relied on? What is happening, and how is it going to affect us? And they begin to pray, to glorify God, and they acknowledge that "a great prophet has risen among us" and "God has visited his people" (Luke 7:16).

Prophets usually don't bring good news to most of us. They confront, condemn, and point out injustice — all that disrupts society and mocks God's goodness. Most people are afraid of prophets, because they disrupt our life and relationships, especially if they have power over life and death. They must be reckoned with, not ignored. To say that a great prophet has arisen in our midst is not a great compliment, because prophets are not generally accepted, loved, or honored. They are feared and rejected by those in power, in established positions and authority. Yet they do bring good news to a specific group. They expose death and needless suffering in society and bring hope and the promise of life to those most in need of life: the poor, the oppressed, the lost ones, the forgotten ones in a society that is running along smoothly, efficiently, and apparently just fine, thank you. A prophet is like a grain of sand in society, but oh, what a grain of sand can do when it is dropped in the mechanism of a very precise timepiece or computer. A prophet drops into a society and all is disrupted, stopped. All life and the way it's "supposed to be" has been stopped in the presence of this man Jesus. To be visited by God means that everything is upside-down. God visits, and there is judgment. God visits, and everything changes. God visits, and they know that something has happened and the word spreads — he is now incredibly well known and famous.

What about those carrying the bier, the pall bearers? The child had died; they had washed and prepared him for burial. They were carrying him out to bury him. What would they have been thinking? They would have been questioning everything Jesus did. Death and everything that touches death is unclean. Rituals of purification are necessary whenever someone has to deal with death. God is the God of the living, not of the dead in the Jewish community. Anything that reeks of death is not of God. And Jesus touched the bier, touched death, and so stopped them all in their tracks. To disrupt the way things are, Jesus touches death, touches all the things that others avoid, refuse to look at, to deal with. Jesus shows us clearly what we must do—to whom we must attend.

What of the child on the bier? Although dead, he hears the voice of Jesus commanding him to arise. He awakes from not being. His spirit returns and answers the voice that called it forth. Did he talk to Jesus? Ask him who he was? Thank him? Was he disoriented and confused? Or, for the first time, did he know who he was? And Jesus gives him back to his mother. He reestablishes that relationship—of son to mother, of son to widowed mother. What was the relationship like now? Or what was it like before and how has it now changed? She is a widow, and he is her only son. He is her lifeline, her support, her connection to the community. The law stipulates that a firstborn son care for his widowed mother until he was thirty years of age. When this child, this son died, she died. She lost all connection to the community, to society. She would have been utterly alone and dead, no rights, no resources, no life in the city. When Jesus gives the child back to her, he gives her back her life, her future, her meaning, and her possibility for a life with dignity, with companionship in the society as it exists. He has saved two lives.

Jesus has pity on the widow and her desperate situation, not only her immediate grief and loss but all that it entails in her society. What would it mean to know that you were given life so that another could live as well? What would it feel like to live knowing that your life is intimately and always connected to the well-being and existence of another, and that is why you are alive now? What would it be like to have God, Jesus, give us to someone else for life? We have other phrases for it: "given in marriage" and "giving a daughter's hand in marriage." Those who engendered life now give it to another to protect and cherish. We give people to each other for nurturing, for life, for honor and trust. We give the catechumens to their sponsors to learn life in the community of Christians. What was the experience now of life for the young man? He was brought back to life to give birth and life to his mother. He is bound forever to one who is helpless in the existing society. It is the reversal of normal life. Instead of the mother giving birth to the child, it is the child that gives life to the mother. Resurrection life comes with enormous responsibility and never-ending connections. God gives us life precisely so we can go back to the community to take care of those in dire need.

What of the widow? She has just lost her only son. She is thinking, that her life is over. Who is going to take care of her? She is walking out to bury her son and bury her own life. She is walking. She has no rights. She is alone, according to Jewish law as alone as any beggar, stranger, foreigner on the streets. Even though she walks out with her neighbors, it is unlikely that any one of them will invite her in, take care of her, and assume responsibility for her future. She knows that she is now on her own. This is why Jesus pities her. Her child has died. That is a usual part of life. It will happen to all of us. But what is not usual, not normal, and not acceptable to Jesus and to God is what individuals, communities — even communities who claim to be believers — do in the face of death and isolation. Jesus pities her. That word arises again and again in the gospels to describe Jesus' reaction to others' experience of injustice and needless suffering, suffering that is continued and made worse by others' choices and insensitivities and refusal to look at what is happening and change so that others might have a chance at life, more life, any life. Pity — that emotion that reveals great sadness, even enough to make one ill, sick, sick enough to throw up at what is happening. This is not life, not the way God intended things to be. It deeply distresses Jesus, and it makes him angry. The other side of pity is anger, anger at people's insensitivity and callousness in the face of another's pain and need. It is pity that allows Jesus to raise the widow of Naim's son from the dead and so bring two people back to life in the presence of people who could help and do not choose to, people who do not even think to change the way society and they treat one another in distress.

The mourners, her neighbors and friends and distant relatives accompany her on her way to death. They go through the ritual of shared grief, planning to go to the cemetery, to the ritual meal, and then to go home, go about their ways.

But what does Jesus do? He stops them. He touches the bier — he puts himself in the same place as she is — outside the community, outside the pale. He freely puts himself alongside her in the place of contamination. That is enough to stop everyone. And she will be remembered for all ages by the Christian community, not because of anything she has done, but because of the great things that God has done for her. Like Mary. Mary, who in all of life lived only for him, living on his word, his truth, his hope for the future. The son sustained the life of his widowed mother. Jesus does not begin his public ministry until after the death of John the Baptist, until after he is thirty years old. He fulfills the Law that requires the firstborn son to care for his widowed mother — giving her his life. The kingdom of heaven, the proclamation of the Good News to the world waits on a woman, waits on a widow. Even as Jesus dies, he thinks of — his mother, who will once again be in jeopardy, alone and without recourse; and so, Jesus gives his mother to John, his youngest disciple, and she is taken into his house. Mary is cared for, given a future, a place in the community, even as Jesus dies. He does for a widowed woman with an only child what his Father will do for him. Even in death he reminds his community of the importance of widows, the forgotten ones, and the poor, the ones on the fringe of his community, among his friends. Certain relationships are stronger than blood in this community of Jesus. Certain people must be taken care of tenderly because of their honored remembrance by God. We are friends of God only when we are their friends, their succor in need, and their hope for a life now and in the future. We live to take care of others in the community in need. Life is given back to us in baptism so that we can take care of them. That is the reason for life in Jesus' community.

In Luke's gospel we are remembered not so much because of blood ties, but because of our association with the poor and the praise we give to God — in imitation of Mary, the one who sings the Magnificat. Our identity is bound up with the poor and the oppressed and how God does great things in us on their behalf. Mary is our model, and this story of the widow and her son echoes this coming to belief and this call to serve.

Mary believes the word of the Lord. Her first reaction to the
announcement of God's entrance into her life is that she is
deeply troubled. Her whole life is disrupted, and her first
response to the news is to ask questions. In some ways Mary
is much like the young man brought to life by the word of
her son. She awakes and submits her entire life to the word
proclaimed to her—"Be it done unto me according to your
Word"—and she sets off to make the incarnation happen. The
young man hears the word of the Lord and arises to live
another life, a life so his widowed mother may have life. The
word of God disrupts everyone's life, all who hear it. It sounds
us out, and it resounds in our lives forever after. Association
with the poor is mandated by the Word of God, and we will
be remembered for what God does in us for them.

Jesus saw a woman, a widow in the larger context of a
society that cared nothing for her, a woman lost and forsaken,
soon to be excluded from the life of the community and city.
Jesus saw her—a widow with no support system, a woman
in grief, and he saw the effects of a system that would do
nothing economically, socially, religiously, or politically to
help her and he had pity on her. He saw a figure, an unknown
person with no name, no life that was to be valued, not a
human being that others would change their lives to help.
She had a lot to cry about, to weep over. And yet, Jesus' first
words are: "Do not cry." In the older translations he calls her
"woman," an honor, giving her life and dignity in the first
word he addresses to her. This seeing revolts Jesus—that
human beings are treated like garbage, leftovers, useless. This
seeing of unnecessary suffering and death also infuriates
Jesus. This seeing makes Jesus stop the reality, interrupt reality, and birth something new. That is what his presence does
in the world of suffering and death. "Don't cry for yourself";
this is not to be accepted. It is to be stopped.

The funeral procession has interrupted Jesus on the way
to somewhere and that interruption calls forth from him
strong emotion, revulsion, and the power of resurrection.
New life, birth, hope, relationship to another in service, hon-
oring the poor, acts of mercy, and acts that resist death and
defy the injustice of the system and of an individual's accep-

tance of this death-dealing reality happen on the way to somewhere else. They interrupt all that we intend to do and take priority. Anyone, any unknown, any lost and forgotten person, anyone cast aside and not considered human and so to be embraced with care and mercy calls forth the power of God and resurrection in Jesus.

What of his followers? There was a saying in the early Christian church: "It is a better thing to feed the poor than to raise someone from the dead." There was an acknowledgment of the dire need to express life, to give and sustain life rather than anything else, even bringing back from the dead someone who had died of natural causes. This resurrection story focuses on the widow, who God in Jesus will not allow to suffer because of the lack of concern of her neighbors and her community and her religious group. The uncaring must stop. Resurrection is the response to injustice and its terrible humiliating death-grip on individuals because of our selfishness and lack of compassion.

We, the followers of Jesus, who have known resurrection in baptism and forgiveness in being saved, must bring others back from the dead and practice resurrection and raising others from the dead. Once in a parish mission when I was studying this scripture with a large group, someone called out harshly, "Have *you* ever brought someone back from the dead?" I had been saying that life happens when we are interrupted, and that some of the most powerful acts of resurrection happen to the least likely people; that we are the people of resurrection and hope, called to live passionately and compassionately with others, to defy death, to forgive, and to bring others back into the community, to do something that is life-giving, that fights death and needless suffering. And then this challenge from the back of the church.

My response was "Yes." I went on to say, "Every time I bring hope into a situation, every time I bring joy that shatters despair, every time I forgive others and give them back dignity and the possibility of a future with me and others in the community, every time I listen to others and affirm them and their life, every time I speak the truth in public, every time I confront injustice—yes—I bring people back from the dead.

Yes." When we do this, it doesn't necessarily bring others to belief, as this story attests. The report spreads around, and Jesus becomes more famous, but not everyone responds with belief in him and his way of life. Jesus doesn't change the system—only the lives of two individuals. This individual practice of compassion and resurrection is crucial to the life of a believer and the community. It is we who change, who alter our realities and make a place, a space, for others to come forth.

Jesus interrupts his journey, his life, for an unknown woman. We are the resurrection community, called to make abundant life for any person we can, anyone we meet in our journeys, to practice acts of mercy for individuals, especially the poorest and forgotten. Every act of compassion is an act that protests injustice; every act that gives life destroys death. We exist for others, to live in hope and to stand against injustice by giving life to another. The child in the story will die again, and the woman will die, but our lives are to proclaim life, even if it puts us in the same group as those who suffer needlessly. One person—poor, rejected, ostracized—what we do for that person we do for the person of Christ, the poor man of God in our midst. Jesus' community is to act on behalf of these *anawim*—it is one of the characteristics of Jesus' life and his followers' lives in the world.

Jesus' words, "Arise, get up!," confront death. And there is death inside each of us, his community, our society and systems and institutions.

Jesus aligns himself with those who are touched by death and suffering, unnecessary suffering that reeks of death; he reaches out and touches it to stop it. There are things to grieve over and mourn and weep and cry over, and there are things that cannot be tolerated, things we are not to waste time weeping over. Death reveals the need for God, for life, and for human compassion. It is a wide-open gate. The poor, those who die unnecessarily, who die because of the systemic injustice, who die slowly, without hope and dignity, crying, do so because of our insensitivity and reluctance to change our lives to accommodate them. Yet they are the place of God's greatest revelation—resurrection. This place of privilege is an invitation. We must accommodate the poor in our lives, we must touch them, associate with them, stand with them against the systems and insensitivity. We must stop our lives to have compassion and pity on them, to give them back life any way we know how. We must help them do more than weep at the situations that injustice inflicts on them. Indeed, we must interrupt society, at least to ease this person's desperate situation, if we are the people of resurrection, the followers of Jesus, if we are to praise God for his glory visiting us.

God visits us most assuredly in the poor and invites us, challenges us, to come back from the dead, to leave aside our associations with those things that destroy another or make life more difficult. This story reminds us to have the broadest possible awareness of compassion and life-giving actions and never, never allow a person to suffer more because of our insensitivity and selfishness and lack of awareness of what structures and society do to people, individual people. We need to train ourselves to be aware of people on the street, on corners, in the city, on farms in situations we prefer to ignore. Until we do this, we are not people of resurrection.

A story is told about Nietzsche, a nineteenth-century philologist and philosopher, who greatly admired Christians but never became one. When asked, in his eighties, why he didn't become a Christian after writing about them and the hope they held out for society (*if* they would practice what they believe and preach), he didn't hesitate for a moment. He answered: "For a group of people that claims to believe in resurrection, none of them looks redeemed."

Most people laugh in reaction to that statement—and that is just the point. People who believe in resurrection should have joy—a virtue that calls forth hope from others, elicits laughter, goodness, and a sense of well-being and newness, no matter the situation. It is a sign of the presence of the Spirit, and it is lavishly given away, shared and spread around to all and anyone who needs it. It is very connected to what my Irish nana used to say: "Take yourself lightly, my dear; take others seriously. After all, angels can fly and dance around on the head of a pin because they take themselves so lightly." Marvelous theology from another widow who lived alone for more than forty years after the death of her husband in a fire, yet lived giving life in great measure wherever she went.

Resurrection people love people day to day. They confront them and challenge them, not letting them stew in their self-pity while avoiding change and caring for others. Resurrection people see others in the larger context of society and recognize what happens to them when they are caught in the system and reduced to being half-human. Resurrection people offer compassion and help and change relationships, but they do not change the individuals. They allow them to respond to compassion and hope in their own ways. Resurrection people motivate others to do something new and then leave them on their own to work it out imaginatively and creatively. Resurrection people remember how hard it is to come back from the dead. They live with the uncomfortableness and learn to treasure it as gift from God who keeps interrupting all of us, trying to teach us to honor God. Resurrection people incarnate the presence of Jesus confronting injustice and doing corporal acts of mercy, and so they remind others that God is visiting God's people again — in the poor, in those crying out to us for compassion and pity, in those who don't count. Resurrection people are called to imitate God's action in history and make the Good News come true for the poor. Resurrection people restore life, give back hope, forgive even enemies, walk together with others, restore what is lost, embrace the poor and the suffering. Resurrection people resist the evil in the world, point it out, and side with those who are its victims. Resurrection people know when to touch death and how to deal with death, when to break taboos, when to align themselves with people cast out from society and rejected because of their association with death. Resurrection people are not afraid to break unjust laws, as Jesus did in touching the bier, even when it puts them on the outside. That's a better place, a more human place to be than with the crowd.

The ministry of resurrection people happens on the way to something else. It happens with strangers and the poor, it happens unexpectedly, it happens in the context of the rest of our life. It happens when we have to be aggressive and command certain things to stop, certain people to stop their usual way of doing things. The ministry of resurrection people happens vicariously through others—the son comforting his mother—and it snowballs, connecting people to others. The ministry of resurrection people is a response of necessity to anyone experiencing injustice, a response of pity to those who cry out under that burden of injustice and being forgotten, falling through the cracks. The ministry of resurrection people is attentive to life and how to birth it in every reality and to speak the truth to others who must hear this reality.

The women of the Plaza de Mayo in South America are often remembered when this scripture passage is studied. These women, many of them widowed, lost their children, grandchildren, husbands, friends, and lovers to torture, disappearance, and death, unknown graves and mass burials. They organized and picketed the government publicly with placards and pictures, weeping and singing and petitioning against the authorities. The two founders were women over sixty years of age. When one of them expressed haltingly why she did what she did—it was so dangerous to herself—she said that when her own child disappeared and she was so frantic, so alone, and so isolated and bereft, it was the first time she thought of other women in the same situation, other mothers and daughters, widows, others experiencing pain, and loss. It bound her to all of them, all the unknowns, the faces, the loss, and the injustice of just not knowing and so being forced to grieve and cry. The others gave her strength, power, and the conviction that it must be stopped, it must be confronted, it must be made public so that others and she herself could have life with dignity again.

Both of the women who founded the mothers of the Plaza de Mayo eventually joined the large and swelling ranks of the disappeared, but they are the lifeline and lifeblood of the ones who continue their long litany of remembrance and of presence that will not be forgotten and silenced. They learned in the facing and touching of death, in defiance of the government forces and army, to stop crying, to not accept this as reality, and to expose death for what it is and to name injustice as a crime against all people and God, and to take command of their own lives again. Then no threats, no death, could silence their cry, their voice, and their call to life. Their visits to the Plaza, their visits with tourists and strangers and newspaper reporters reminded the world of what needed to be done, needed to be looked at and seen for what it was. Their visits brought comfort and hope to others in similar situations, and their visits and actions were prophetic words that would not be silenced, even in their disappearances. Those men and women, many of them widows, used this scripture passage often to stir up again their hope, their courage, and their intent to stop death and make society take responsibility for its actions and its lack of justice and compassion. The resurrection became a daily reality, a pattern, and a practice in their lives. It gave them back meaning and joy in the midst of anguish, violence, and the world's insensitivity to their plight, and it gave them justice. Their arising and standing up to death gave life to many around the world. This account of resurrection tells us to break silence, commit ourselves to compassion and protection of life, especially life that is vulnerable. It tells us not to accept situations the way they are, to reject any reality that destroys life, limits life, robs people of dignity, to resist death and give back life, to judge systems and their effects on individuals, and to expose that injustice publicly.

Resurrection says we must stand in solidarity with the poor, all those people who experience life as difficult, and refute anyone that keeps on with life as usual while others suffer. What we do in public, where we stand, what we say is connected intimately to resurrection. Resurrection reveals the prophets among us, those who say no to death and yes to life. It reveals the bitterness that is the aftertaste of injustice and insensitivity. No one is to suffer in basic human needs because of our lack of awareness and reluctance to alter our own behaviors. Dorothy Day said that she decided to become a Catholic when it dawned on her that Jesus' words about bringing life and ever more abundant life into the world, meant not just her, but others as well. We, as community, are to be a sign of resurrection life and its reality and power in the world now, today, here in this city, on this road. We, as community, are to give people back to each other as Jesus gave the woman back her son, as Elijah gave the woman back her son, as God gave Jesus back to us. God still, it seems, likes to visit us in the guise of the poor, the widowed, the orphaned, and the prophet. Perhaps we need to watch the ravens. They may be feeding a prophet hiding in our midst, one who is getting ready to interrupt our lives.

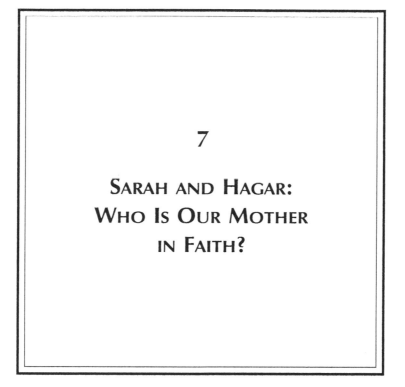

# 7

## SARAH AND HAGAR:
## WHO IS OUR MOTHER
## IN FAITH?

I n the past decades theology has changed, sometimes radically. The experiences of history, of the Vatican Council, of feminism, of equality and education have brought many theologians to examine traditional texts and beliefs more closely, to include women whenever possible, and to change theological and liturgical language to be inclusive and descriptive of both genders' reality. And so, there has been a turn toward fathering and mothering in God and in the church's description of itself.

One of the first debates and marked changes was in talking about Abraham, our father in faith. If we have a father in faith, then we must have a mother in faith as well. So, without much theological study or discussion, Sarah, Abraham's wife and Isaac's mother, became our mother in faith. Even though the choice seems obvious, this approach goes against one of the primary rules to remember in doing feminist theology: women are to be remembered and imitated, not because they are someone's mother or daughter or wife, but on their own terms. Yet the primary reason for Sarah being chosen as our mother in faith was that she was there, conveniently married to Abraham and mother of one of the patriarchs.

In many countries—in Central and South America, in Canada, in England and Ireland, in the United States—I have used the story of Abraham, Sarah, Hagar, Isaac, and Ishmael to look at what makes a woman our mother in faith and how to look at gender issues in theology with some other eyes than contemporary Western ones. Perhaps in our desire to incorporate a woman into our prayers and rituals and modeling of faith, we jumped without looking where we jumped and what we jumped into. We need balance, and we need alternative visions and expressions of belief. We can use a mother in faith, certainly—but is it Sarah? Perhaps a closer look at the stories in Genesis about these people and the interpretations of others might reveal things that are powerfully true, even if they do not immediately fit our Western interpretations of scripture. They may not even serve first-world women's ways of looking at and using texts in their agenda of inclusion — a cultural point of view that is certainly a minority opinion in regard to the sheer number of women in the world. Perhaps Western cultural, educational, and racial biases are showing more than we care to admit in our theologizing. Let us look at the book of Genesis — the collection of stories of our beginnings in faith — and see what the texts and contexts of the stories reveal.

Both for Jews and Christians the Book of Exodus is the source book of liberation, of hope, and of how God intervenes in history and calls forth a people. This process and long story of liberation and freedom begins with Yahweh's response to the cry of the poor, the oppressed, and the slaves in Egypt. This cry rises unceasingly and enduringly, almost without hope, assailing God and God responds with power to this desperate prayer of need. The Jewish midrash describes God leaning down close to earth as a mother would to a child and hearing with a deep ache the pain of the children of Joseph in their land of bondage. It is the image of a mother putting her cheek against the cheek of a sick infant. This book and the catalog of events provides the foundation for much biblical study, even the events of Jesus' passover, provide material for reinterpretation of the original Exodus. And, in more recent times, the Black community has looked to the Exodus as the symbol of the civil rights movement and its long march to freedom.

Today we look again to the ancient stories to shed light on our own histories and struggles. This background, this context, weaves strong threads in contemporary patterns. In fact, so much study has been done on some of the books of the Hebrew scriptures that a distinct picture is emerging on the underside, the back of the original weaving. The picture on the underside is just as rich and intricate in detail and color, perhaps even more powerful in its revelation because it is unexpected and it has been hidden for so long. It is the story of the poor, the cry of the masses that has gone unheard and unacknowledged and unresponded to for so long, and it is the poor themselves that are reweaving and uncovering this design in the midst of persecution and poverty, disappearances and hope. They are reminding the rest of the world and the church of how, in their search for justice, they have found the Spirit's presence in their lives and in the scriptures -- that God has always heard their cry and that their hidden stories have survived underneath the text of the larger stories of faith and salvation history.

It is this time in history and faith that is calling forth the lost and forgotten. They are appearing, not just as another method in theology or another aspect of belief, but as the threads that hold the whole picture together, the threads that have been taken for granted and unnoticed. This is clearly stated in a poem called "Revelation" by Julia Esquivel.*

> The words of the poor
> are knives
> that bury themselves
> in our flesh
> and cut,
> and hurt,
> and draw out
> infection.
> The cry of the poor
> is clear water
> that rinses off our makeup;
> we can let the mask fall.
> The eyes of the poor
> are two mirrors,
> we need not be afraid
> to see ourselves there.
> The nearness of the poor
> reveals Jesus
> excellent Counselor,
> God with us,
> Prince of Peace,

*The Certainty of Spring: Poems by a Guatemalan in Exile (Washington, D.C.: EPICA, 1992). Reprinted with permission.

Fire that burns away
all chaff
and purifies gold!

The poor, the masses of folk in the world and the church, do theology. They do it astutely, for life and death reasons, for hope in the face of terrible evils and destruction, for a dearer life for their children and the earth. And their seeing, their searching of the text is accompanied first by the Spirit and then by those who have gone before them in faith and given their lives. Once we hear them do theology, applying it to their own situations, calling themselves to the cross and denying self and community to seek justice and reconciliation, we can never be the same again. We realize that the act of theologizing is an act of justice, of truth-telling, and of courage in itself in a context of life and death.

This chapter comes out of the privileged experience of the poor teaching me to do theology and to listen to the underside. They remind me that the Spirit hides in the most unlikely places and in places we don't want to find the raging, seeping Spirit—in our enemies, the slaves and cast-offs, and the ones who complicate our life of faith and interrupt our organized and nicely fitting answers. The slave woman Hagar and her firstborn child of Abraham, Ishmael, are the wild cards in the story of Genesis that introduces us to our covenant with God and what faith might mean for the earth and all its people.

The story of Abram and Sarai (their names are changed to Abraham and Sarah after the covenant with Yahweh) starts with a call to leave the land of their ancestors and Abram's father's house and to set out in mystery to a land that God will show them. It is as vague as that, but accompanied by a promise that marks the beginning of a long journey that includes all of us who believe in the Jewish and Christian traditions.

> "*I will make of you a great nation,*
> *and I will bless you;*
> *I will make your name great,*
> *so that you will be a blessing.*

*I will bless those who bless you and curse those who*
    *curse you.*
*All the communities of the earth*
    *shall find blessing in you" (Genesis 12:2-3).*

So the story begins with Abram being directed by the Lord into the future. He is seventy-five when the journey commences. His household passes through the land of Canaan as far as the sacred place at Shechem by the tree of Moreh. And Abram and Sarai take everything with them, including their slaves and possessions. The Lord appears again to Abram and says: "To your descendants I will give this land" (Genesis 12:7). Now begins a time of waiting and learning who this Lord is who makes promises and words come true in ways no one ever thought possible.

The journey continues into Egypt and to Bethel and Ai, where Abram had first built an altar to the Lord. There Lot and Abram part company. We are told that Abram was now very rich in livestock, silver, and gold. There are battles and intrigues, but the Lord returns in a vision to Abram.

*"Fear not, Abram!*
  *I am your shield;*
  *I will make your reward very great."*

*But Abram said: "O Lord GOD, what good will your gifts be, if I keep on being childless and have as my heir the steward of my house, Eliezer? Abram, continued, "See, you have given me no offspring."* . . . *Then the word of the LORD came to him: "No, that one shall not be your heir; your own issue shall be your heir." He took him outside and said: "Look up at the sky and count the stars, if you can. Just so," he added, "shall your descendants be." Abram put his faith in the LORD, who credited it to him as an act of righteousness (Genesis 15:1-6).*

Now the promise begins to take on specific form, in spite of human frailty and seemingly impossible odds. Abram and Sarai are childless; Sarai is barren (a terrible curse in that culture). Yet Abram believes the impossible will happen and leans on the word of the Lord. Faith, an act of righteousness, is credited to him by God!

So now we turn to the story of Sarai, Abram's wife, and Sarai's maidservant Hagar.

> *Abram's wife Sarai had borne him no children. She had, how-ever, an Egyptian maidservant named Hagar. Sarai said to Abram: "The LORD has kept me from bearing children. Have intercourse, then, with my maid; perhaps I shall have sons through her." Abram heeded Sarai's request. Thus, after Abram had lived ten years in the land of Canaan, his wife Sarai took her maid, Hagar the Egyptian, and gave her to her husband Abram to be his concubine. He had intercourse with her, and she became pregnant. When she became aware of her preg-nancy, she looked on her mistress with disdain. So Sarai said to Abram: "You are responsible for this outrage against me. I myself gave my maid to your embrace; but ever since she became aware of her pregnancy, she has been looking on me with disdain. May the LORD decide between you and me!" Abram told Sarai: "Your maid is in your power. Do to her whatever you please." Sarai then abused her so much that Hagar ran away from her (Genesis 16:1-6).*

The story is about two women in conflict: one is rich, the mistress of the household, but barren and growing old; the other is obviously younger, perhaps beautiful, fertile, and a slave. Sarai is Israelite, and Hagar is Egyptian, perhaps bought during their time in Egypt when Sarai lived in the palace. We tend to identify with Sarai and not with Hagar, who, annoy-ingly, keeps being inserted into the story and complicating matters by her behavior and the events surrounding her and Sarai. After all, Hagar is a slave, a maid, a piece of property that can be bought and sold, given away, or treated inhu-manely; she is even given over to the head of the household by her mistress to have children for her. Her own body and her offspring aren't even hers. What does she have? Even her dignity is worn thin in such a situation. (Remember, it is the slaves' cries in Egypt that will set in motion the freedom of a whole people when God moves on their behalf). Hagar is an outsider as well as poor and a maid—domestic help that belongs to Sarai forever, unless her mistress decides to set her free. Only Hebrew slaves were set free in the seventh or jubilee years; foreigners stayed slaves. The law gave hope only to Israelites, not to pagans.

Sarai refuses to let things happen in God's own time. She begins to move so that she has some control over who will inherit the name and the possessions and who will care for her in her old age. She gives her servant to Abram (this practice was legal in the area at the time; Rachel and Leah do it also), knowing that any child fathered by Abram is legitimate. And Hagar gets pregnant. The promise is now coming true, a fact, for the child will be the firstborn son of Abram, acceptable but a bit problematic, being of mixed race and part slave.

We are told that as soon as Hagar is pregnant her attitude changes. She begins to treat Sarai with disdain! Whenever this passage is read, reactions are split diametrically, depending on the audience. There is indignation and interpretations of jealousy and pettiness against Hagar among women who are educated and economically stable; there is laughter and delight among poor women.

I once read the story with a group of maids with whom I worked off and on at a local motel. We met on our breaks and read scripture while watching the soaps in between rooms. They were absolutely delighted; they had never heard the story and thought it was great. One woman, an illegal immigrant from El Salvador, said in her halting English: "Oh, now Sarai gets a taste of her own medicine. Now she knows what it's like to be a slave and be treated like dirt all the time. Serves her right. She doesn't like it—well, we don't either. We don't live just to clean toilets, iron, and clean up after others and to be pushed around." I was stunned, and yet it made perfect sense.

Hagar's being pregnant with Abram's first born, who will not even belong to her but to Abram and Sarai, gave her a taste of freedom, of hope, of liberation. She is now Abram's concubine, so there is the possibility of being set free, of having a life with a son and the man who has taken her and needed her. She knows there is a difference between living in slavery and living. She begins to feel like a human being. But Sarai is enraged and blames Abram for what is going on. She tells him to do something. By this she is insinuating that he should follow the laws (the code of Hammurabi) and assert his place as head of the household and her rights as wife against Hagar. Abram does. He hands over Hagar into Sarai's hands, to "her power," and says to do whatever she pleases with her.

No wonder Hagar runs away! Again, the women at the motel cheered Hagar on. They all agreed that rather than live in humiliation and hatred and persecution it was better to run away. Having tasted a hope for a better life, she has to fight back or run away. Hagar rebels against her unjust and inhuman treatment by Sarai and goes into the desert.

> *The LORD's messenger found her by a spring in the wilderness, the spring on the road to Shur, and he asked, "Hagar, maid of Sarai, where have you come from and where are you going?" She answered, "I am running away from my mistress, Sarai." But the LORD's messenger told her: "Go back to your mistress and submit to her abusive treatment. I will make your descendants so numerous," added the LORD's messenger, "that they will be too many to count." "Besides," the LORD's messenger said to her:*

> *"You are now pregnant and shall bear a son; you shall name him Ishmael, For the LORD has heard you, God has answered you.*

> *He shall be a wild ass of a man, his hand against everyone, and everyone's hand against him; In opposition to all his kin shall he encamp."*

> *To the LORD who spoke to her she gave a name, saying, "You are the God of Vision"; she meant, "Have I really seen God and remained alive after my vision?" That is why the*

*well is called Beer-lahai-roi. It is between Kadesh and Bered.*

*Hagar bore Abram a son, and Abram named the son whom Hagar bore him Ishmael. Abram was eighty-six years old when Hagar bore him Ishmael (Genesis 16:7-16).*

The messenger of the Lord comes to Hagar in the desert with a question: "Where have you come from and where are you going?" The tradition in Israel and in the Hebrew scriptures is that there is no difference between the messengers of God and God. Hagar is visited by God! She is pregnant, near a spring, and God blesses her, gives her a promise, and names her child before its birth. This story has all the details and form of an annunciation event that must be noticed and taken into account in the overall tradition.

Hagar is told to go back to her mistress and suffer through abuse and mistreatment. The motel maids cried out loudly against this, and then one of them said, "She has to. She has to think of her child, not herself." There is a time to rebel, and a time to run, and a time to endure. These are realistic and cold-blooded and strong reactions—for the poor the story makes sense. What followed at the motel were their own stories—of being maids in the houses of the rich, of getting pregnant by the husband or father and being thrown out, of running away, of being treated as old clothes the rich get tired of—not even given away but thrown out in the garbage.

These women love Hagar. They are full of hope when God comes to her and names her son Ishmael—wild and free and in opposition to his kin. Hagar and Ismael highlight Abram and Sarai, the masters of the house, the rich and selfish and dominant who are sure that they are right, who live their personal lives of faith with God and yet treat their slaves without justice. The maids read the story in Spanish to their children and cousins and aunts, and they talk about it for weeks. God comes to the poor and the desperate—the maids—and talks with them just as God talks with Abram and "important" people. I tell them that Hagar is the only woman in the Hebrew scriptures who sees God—and she sees him twice! They smile and say nothing, but the knowing look on their faces is old. Their faces are all young, in their teens and twenties, but they have seen the desert and the oppression and know the story of Hagar is their own story.

Hagar sees God and lives. She can't believe it. Tradition said that if a person saw God, the person died from the encounter. And she gives God a name! The God of Vision — of far seeing, of the future, of knowing the present and taking note of her, just a maid, a pregnant slave, and an Egyptian, not even a Jew! God cares about everyone, but especially about anyone thrown out, thrown away, or desperate enough to run from violence, humiliation, and brutality, even domestic brutality.

Then we find that Abraham (his new name now) is told that Sarah will bear a son (at ninety). He has Ishmael and all his slaves and members of his household circumcised as a sign of the covenant and his faithfulness and belief in the words of God. God further blesses Ishmael to Abraham: "I hereby bless him. I will make him fertile and will multiply him exceedingly. He shall become the father of twelve chieftains, and I will make of him a great nation. But my covenant I will maintain with Isaac, whom Sarah shall bear to you by this time next year" (Genesis 17:20-21). Ishmael is thirteen years old at the time of this promise.

When the messengers come to Abraham and announce that a child will be born to Sarah, Sarah laughingly dismisses it all.

> But the LORD said to Abraham: "Why did Sarah laugh and say, 'Shall I really bear a child, old as I am?' Is anything too marvelous for the LORD to do? At the appointed time, about this time next year, I will return to you, and Sarah will have a son." Because she was afraid, Sarah dissembled, saying "I didn't laugh." But he said, "Yes, you did" (Genesis 18:13-15).

Sarah reacts to the fulfillment of the covenant promise with laughter and is caught. Nine months later she has her child; Isaac, whose name means "she laughed!" The covenant has now been fulfilled, not by Sarah's wiles and maneuvering, but by Yahweh's word that does impossible things.

But we're not done with Sarah and Hagar yet. Sarah will not let things lie. The story gets ugly.

*Sarah noticed the son whom Hagar the Egyptian had borne to Abraham playing with her son Isaac; so she demanded of Abraham: "Drive out that slave and her son! No son of that slave is going to share the inheritance with my son Isaac!" Abraham was greatly distressed, especially on account of his son Ishmael. But God said to Abraham: "Do not be distressed about the boy or about your slave woman. Heed the demands of Sarah, no matter what she is asking of you; for it is through Isaac that descendants shall bear your name. As for the son of the slave woman, I will make a great nation of him also, since he too is your offspring."*

*Early the next morning Abraham got some bread and a skin of water and gave them to Hagar. Then, placing the child on her back, he sent her away. As she roamed aimlessly in the wilderness of Beer-sheba, the water in the skin was used up. So she put the child down under a shrub, and then went and sat down opposite him, about a bowshot away; for she said to herself, "Let me not watch the child die." As she sat opposite him, he began to cry. God heard the boy's cry, and God's messenger called to Hagar from heaven: "What is the matter, Hagar? Don't be afraid; God has heard the boy's cry in this plight of his. Arise, lift up the boy and hold him by the hand; for I will make of him a great nation." Then God opened her eyes, and she saw a well of water. She went and filled the skin with water, and then let the boy drink.*

*God was with the boy as he grew up. He lived in the wilderness and became an expert bowman, with his home in the wilderness of Paran. His mother got a wife for him from the land of Egypt (Genesis 21:9-21).*

Note that there are *two* stories of Hagar in the desert. In one, the child is either thirteen or fourteen; in the other he is just two or three. It doesn't really matter; in either case he is a child seen as a threat to the existing structure. Sarah's reaction to the child Ishmael is cold-blooded and ruthless, and her actions toward Hagar speak of jealousy and rage. She keeps referring to them as "that slave woman" and "that son of a slave"—who happens to be Abraham's firstborn son! Yet Abraham does what Sarah says, ignoring his own feelings;

God promises to care for them, even though Sarah makes as sure as she can that they will both die or disappear from her life forever. Sarah's behavior betrays an inhumanity and insensitivity and selfishness that is appalling, no matter who she is as Abraham's wife and the mother of Isaac the patriarch.

On the other hand, Hagar once again meets God face to face and is told that God has heard the boy's cry and seen her destitution and danger. God gives her water, sight, and courage to help the boy grow up—even to providing a wife for him from his own people, the Egyptians. This Hagar is a most resourceful woman and is both mother and father to her child, Ishmael. God does not let her and the boy die in the desert, just as God will not let the chosen people die in the desert later on in history. God is the God of slaves and Egyptians and foreigners and those not wanted and feared by the Israelites, but it will take a long time and many stories to teach God's people that reality. Nonetheless, the examples and the stories begin early, at the beginning, in Genesis. God is just as concerned about the hopes and dreams and future of those who are not Israelites as about those chosen to stand out among the other nations. All nations and all peoples are God's children (the echo of Jesus in the gospel with good news to the poor—any and all poor).

Those in oppression and poverty today hear the cries in the story of Abraham and recognize their own voices, their own rejection of slavery, servitude, and inequality. When asked by the messenger of the Lord, "Where are you from and where are you going?" all Hagar can answer is, "I'm running away from my mistress." I'm running away from slavery, from a life without a future, without hope and without dignity; a life without tenderness and friendship. When she is instructed to return to an abusive situation, she obeys in order to guarantee a life, a name, and a place for her son, her child who is half slave and half free. The second time in the desert she is even more desperate—she cannot bear to see her child suffering and dying, and the words she hears begins: "Fear not"—the opening words to ease another woman at the beginning of her child's sojourn into the world. Mary, the mother of Jesus, will know Hagar's agony of watching her child die cruelly and unjustly because of others and will remain steadfast in faith and trust in the word of God.

So Hagar stands up, stands up for her child, her life, and her future, her hope and freedom and the vision of what is to come. Even in her vision she could never have imagined the extent and power of the vision of Yahweh, which would be revealed in another woman's child looked down upon and rejected, Jesus, son of Mary, wife of Joseph. Like Hagar, Mary will spend long years alone with her child, after the death of Joseph, her protection in society and Jewish culture. Hagar is like many women who are refugees and immigrants and illegal aliens, barely tolerated or even persecuted and hunted down. She reminds us as well of their sisters, mothers, cousins, and friends, left behind and struggling alone to care for their families because of the death or disappearance of their husbands, brothers, and children. The realities of injustice, slavery, oppression, racism, and hatred are still common in the world.

But the story ends well. Hagar, her child Ishmael, and their descendants are free—free of Israelite slavery and free from fear and domination. Theirs is a mini-version of the larger story to come when Yahweh will hear the cry of a whole people in bondage and lean down to their cries as God leans down to this woman and child, unwanted and thrown out in the desert to die. Ishmael (the name means "God hears") is the hope, hidden but potent and waiting on the time of God to burst forth as the hope of all slaves and oppressed peoples. This God who hears the cry of the poor will not fit into any neat categories of theology and meaning. The woman Mary in her song of freedom, the Magnificat, will describe herself as lowly, humble, the servant, the handmaid of God—like Hagar—and she will sing of the turning upside-down of society, where the lowly will be raised to high places and the rich cast aside and thrown out empty-handed. This will become the faith and fervent belief of all the children of Abraham, our ancestors in faith, who uphold Israel throughout all the generations of history in the long wait for the Messiah.

Gustavo Gutiérrez has described the poor and the oppressed as co-creators with God of history; they too are the children of God discovering divine love, Spirit, and courage in their sufferings and deaths. They reveal a face of God long covered, the God of solicitude for those in dire need and those who stand in solidarity with others who simply endure faithfully the effects of injustice and misery that are the consequences of sinful structures and selfish human choices.

The poor are raised by those who survive — often their mothers and sisters and aunts — to be strong and courageous and faithful. They have to be! Today the poor are learning self-confidence and self-worth; they are discovering they do have a voice, both as individuals and with others. Catechists, delegates of the word, leaders of base communities, organizers for justice, all interpret the scriptures and come to believe that their stories are hidden in the larger story as the privileged place of God's revelation. Things missed the first time around or lost in the shuffle are now surfacing stronger and clearer than ever before in the voice of the Spirit. The poor are still humble, but now they are also feisty, determined, and strong-willed on behalf of justice and their children's lives.

The presence of God is among them, among the maids and house-servants and farm workers and day laborers and refugees and displaced and those widowed by war and made outcast by rape and abuse. They know that God's way is not one of easy solutions or magical moments and immediate change. They know from hard experience that radical change takes time; hard work, and solidarity — and the lives and deaths of many people — before anyone even notices their struggle for an identity and happiness, let alone cares to help them in that journey to dignity. They rely on the protection and care of God for years, decades, because no one else comes to their rescue. They are open to the signs of life, of water and nourishment and hope around them. Their history and coming to consciousness are like Hagar's — God has opened their eyes and given them sight. God sustains them as they endure and grow stronger in faith and in the experience of the promise that God is with them and hears their cries.

What makes a woman of faith? Is it giving birth in a chain of miraculous events, events that are taken out of the context of a life and other relationships? Or is a woman of faith constituted by a discipline of hope, of trust in God, in refusal to give up, in courage, in leaning on the word of God because there is no one else to lean on or aid her and children? What makes a woman of faith? Is it being the wife of the father of the child of the promise by blood and race and religion? Or is a woman of faith not defined by boundaries of culture, religion, race, and economic status but rather characterized by steadfast clinging to life, protecting the unborn and young of her family, even to the point of enduring abuse and mistreatment humbly so that the child of her promise has a chance at life? What makes a woman of faith? Is it association and bloodlines in the community of those called the people of God, those who will become the Israelites? Or is a woman of faith anyone, even an outsider, a slave, a rebellious woman who resists servitude and is given the sight of God, the word of God, her own covenant and vision of the future, and the ability to survive in spite of some of the other chosen people? Perhaps we do have a mother in faith, but not Sarah, the bitter, unbelieving, and cynical woman driven by jealousy and fear, a woman who does not see her slave even as a woman like herself but as something useful for a time for her own security. Perhaps our mother in faith is Hagar, the Egyptian slave woman, mother of Ishmael, the firstborn of Abraham, our father in faith—not because she's anyone's mother or concubine or slave or maid, but because she is poor and oppressed, reliant on God, the one God chose to give hope to all the struggling peoples of the world unnoticed, unappreciated, and thrown away carelessly, even by people who are learning faith in God, but are slow and stubborn about sharing that faith in justice with the rest of humankind.

Often in discussions of this story, someone says, "Well, it seems Sarah is still treating Hagar the same way today. Things haven't changed much." Maybe the issue isn't just feminism in opposition to patriarchy. Maybe the deeper sin is racism and classism. After all, Hagar and Sarah are both women, sisters, and still Sarah treats Hagar as dirt, as not human, certainly not as an equal in any regard. Sarah treats Hagar as many women say men treat them. The real issue is about power, security, and privilege—control over one's own life.

This story is disturbing. It causes many, women especially, to "disassemble" — to use the word that describes Sarah when she gets caught laughing about the ways of God in her life and history. This story disassembles many of the newly acceptable ideas of theology and interpretation of the scriptures in mainstream theology done by women in the First World. Ana María Tepedino, a theologian from Brazil, writes:

Feminist theology in the Third World arises out of the realities of daily life. It goes beyond the experience of oppression. It goes beyond the experience of God. It goes beyond the struggle for justice. Always it includes the "practice of tenderness." We women know the cultural oppression of a patriarchal, male-chauvinist society; we have lived on the underside of power and authority. Yet we seek to create brotherly and sisterly relationships among all people. Theological reflection from a woman's point of view wishes to make its voice heard as a service to all those alienated from society. A woman, by her constitution, seems always to be extending herself, carrying people — through her experience of faith, of prayer, of life. She feels the impetus to overcome individualism and hears the call to community experience. She meditates on the things of the heart and opens herself fully to communion — hence her sensitivity to the needs of others.

This sensitivity to the pain of others builds a capacity for compassion — suffering and feeling with others, being in solidarity with them, being more open to their problems, understanding the values of sharing in the struggle for better living conditions. Through all of this, women transmit the faith characterized by the struggle for justice. Theirs is a faith marked by love — love close (sharing bread with the hungry) or love at a distance (working to change unjust structures). Women do theology with a passion.*

*Ana María Tepedino, "Martha's Passion: A Model for Theological Liberation," *The Other Side* (July-August 1988), pp. 22-25.

Many of the liberation theologians of Latin America, including women theologians, are convinced that women's oppression is determined above all by their social situation, their position in society that determines the kind of oppression they live under. This differs from one group of women to another. The struggle to break out of oppression does not begin with institutions but with poor women who are forming groups of twos and threes, trying to break out of the cycle of misery, poverty, no choices, and no futures. They struggle to change their own immediate lives, to acquire basic necessities, but also to change society's consciousness of why they have to live in this way. They often seek to change the consciousness of other women who share their same oppression and women in other sectors of society who have more power in the institutional structures of economics, politics, academics, and the church.

The immediate environment of culture and economics defines more brutally what oppression is. Anyone can aggravate the situation and be insensitive to it and to their plight — other men and other women of higher social classes and education and culture. Women employers, women professors and writers, women with the freedom to do research and travel, women who hire other women to clean their houses and take care of their children are often blind to the treatment of poor women, including the ones they are bound to, and especially to the plight of women of color. Poor women do theology differently from well-educated, comfortable, and wealthy women of a culture that dominates the cultures of minorities (who happen to be the majority of people and of women worldwide). The voice of the poor, especially poor women, is often unheard by sisters better off, more secure, and benefiting individually from the dominant culture's systems and priorities.

Many poor women do not believe that gender is the basic problem. It is more complicated than that — as the issues between Sarah and Hagar remind us. It is an interlocking set of oppressions. Theology done primarily by women who see gender as the main focus of oppression often begins with assumptions that a majority of women do not accept. Further it ignores crucial areas of immediate concern—food, shelter, survival, health care, basic literacy skills, jobs, and so on. A world, a church, and a theology dominated by anyone, male or female, is just that—domination. Sarah dominates as thoroughly on an individual level as patriarchy does on a systemic level. Sarah is just as dangerous and disheartening as the system, perhaps even more so because of the common bond that is destroyed in the encounter—that of sisterhood.

Sexism is a problem, but so are individualism, materialism, consumerism, capitalism, racism, and politics and economics that allow for domination. We can be in opposition to one, but fail to question the effects of the others on our thoughts, our theology, and our methods and lifestyles. The issue of individualism, for example, of a woman making decisions about her own body, her children, her identity, without the context of a community, of a group that holds her accountable beyond her personal desires is incomprehensible within Christianity and the universal aspects of liberation. What frees one does not necessarily contribute to the freedom of anyone else and may set back many others struggling for mere survival with gracefulness.

Liberation, of its nature, is communal. God hears the cry of Hagar and her child in the desert, but as the story grows in power God hears the cry of God's people in Egypt and bends to them, and finally in Jesus God answers the cry of all the poor, of all people marginalized, ignored, or treated unjustly.

Often I hear the hope, the suggestion that women who are better off, more educated, more individual in their concerns and not necessarily tied to women who are poor might be more humble, quieter, and learn to listen and accept the experience of poor men and women. I also hear the hope that the better-off would be willing to change their fervently-held beliefs to accommodate radical personal change and conversion in their own lives, both in theory and practice. The central concerns of those in a dominant culture, however worthy, such as issues of power within the church, ordination, women's access to ministry and decision-making, issues of sexual identity, orientation, pro-choice stances, and so on are not the focal issues for those in other cultures, races, and classes in the church, whose more pressing concerns are redistribution of land, housing, education, health care, and responses to violence and abuse. The issues of poverty, slavery, servitude, dominance, and collusion with a culture that encourages individualism, materialism, and personal power must be criticized and condemned. The ethics and practices of individuals and societies and churches and nations must be examined through the lens of discipleship, the virtue of poverty, and the practice of making and building community support and justice especially for the weakest members of society: male or female, young or elderly, whatever race or social position. Spirituality must be based on the Spirit that blows where it will, not necessarily in acceptable places among those already in power. It must be a spirituality that recognizes and rejoices in the reality that at this point in history the face of the poor is the privileged place of revelation of God, and that the poor are a gift given to the church and the world to evangelize it and call it to fullness of life with all peoples. The option for the poor is not really an option; it is a fundamental imperative of the Spirit of God, the God of Vision, the God of Hagar and Ishmael as well as Abraham, Sarah, and Isaac. The reading of the scriptures by the poor and their interpretations may make us "disassemble," and confront our own biases, call us to account for our lives in very personal responses to injustice and individual people, and convict us of insensitivity to others, callousness in our own endeavors, and attitudes of racism, selfishness, and self-righteousness.

In the tradition of the Jewish midrash, the Torah, the scriptures are black fire written on white fire—sparking furious power and insight, allowing the Spirit to rush through any word, phrase, story, or text without warning. The scriptures are inspired both textually and contextually, and those who read the scriptures with the Spirit will alter the interpretation. The interpretation that makes us most human and most divine, most aware of and careful of others—*that* is the interpretation that is most true, most holy, and most to be listened to, taken to heart, and put into practice. What is sacred is people—the poor, the weak, the least, the ones that keep

interrupting our set practices of belief and religion, the unexpected face of God stumbling into our camps and tents and
saying, "Excuse us, but we are here too. Have you forgotten
about us in your spirituality, your arranging of the world, and
your place with God?"

Hagar's story is not what we are used to seeing. It jolts, it
disarms, it rages with pain and rejection and loneliness, and
it questions what needs to be questioned: What ties us
together? What binds us as one? What is our religion? Is it
the word of the Lord, the imperious command to life, life ever
more abundantly for all human beings following in the vision
of Jesus? Is it faith, not just in one people, but in all people,
any people, especially those who most need faith and a
response to their cry to God? Our mother in faith, Hagar,
teaches us that faith breaks all boundaries of sin, of injustice,
of race, religion, social class, nations, and structures. Faith is
an undying hope in freedom, obedience to the vision and the
word of God, and fierce tenderness toward the weak, the
poor, the slaves whose faces reveal Yahweh, Jesus, and the
Spirit. Faith is hearing the cries of the poor, siding with them,
giving them vision and a future. Faith is knowing that no one
can be allowed to remain abused and treated inhumanely by
anyone else. Faith is relying on God when there is no one
else there, not even those who claim to be people of faith.

Our mother in faith is a black slave woman who refused
to be humiliated, who saw God, who knew in her flesh a
promise and the reality that God is revealed to those most
desperate as well as those chosen as God's people. Our
mother in faith is a woman stumbling in the desert while her
child clings to her for life, who is befriended by God when
everyone else abandons her. Our mother in faith foreshadows
the woman Mary, who will sing of freedom and be great not
simply because she is the mother of Jesus, but because she is
the first to believe in the word that was spoken to her.

If we start rewriting prayers, perhaps they should honor
Abraham and Hagar, our forerunners in faith, our unsus-
pecting ancestors, who stumbled along the road to freedom
and knew the mercy of God face to face. Maybe Hagar, the
maidservant, is given to us in this age to confront us with

injustice, servitude, personal weakness, and lack of faith, especially among those who are well-off, sure of themselves theologically, and able to manipulate the law, the culture, the language, the system, and relationships for their own ends while still missing the heart of the matter—compassion and freedom for all peoples. Hagar is rebelling against her mistress still, but this time perhaps, with grace, her mistress will listen and learn how to embrace her as a sister, a child of God, a woman seeking to live with dignity. This time Sarah may share some of her wealth, status, and privilege with Hagar in justice.

Perhaps women along with men must learn in their flesh what the tenderness of God is. Perhaps Hagar, our mother in faith, reminds us that being human is the first and critical reality of faith. Perhaps the next time the messenger of the Lord asks Hagar, "Where are you from and where are you going?" she won't answer that she is running away from her mistress, from another woman. Perhaps it's time to change the story and to change any theology so that it's done together by all women—rich or poor, slave or free, whatever nation or race or religion—and with men. Perhaps that will be humankind's best theology ever.

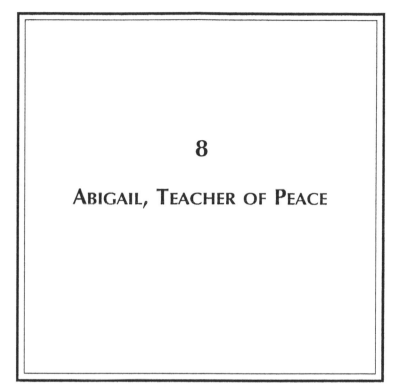

# 8

# ABIGAIL, TEACHER OF PEACE

W henever I talk about the woman named Abigail, there are blank stares on most peoples' faces. Who is she? Her story is found in the First Book of Samuel.

Abigail lives in a time of confrontation, war, violence, and upheaval. Israel is in the early stages of the kingdom, and Saul is king. But Saul's behavior and lack of faith have displeased Yahweh. Saul is losing ground and power in his own kingdom, and he is also fighting a war, something of a national liberation war in Canaan. When the Israelites came into the promised land, it was already occupied. The stories of the violent taking of the land occupy much of early Jewish history from Joshua through the books of Kings. Israel, it seems, is always at war, either keeping its hold on its territory or engaged in other battles. The god of early Israel in Canaan seems more like a general leading an army than even a king ruling the land. Indeed, the name Yahweh Sabaoth means Lord God of hosts—with all its allusions to an army and an invading horde. The Israelites are warriors, defenders of the honor of God and the land they acquire in their battles. They have been liberated from the Egyptians, but they are no longer simply desert nomads. They are becoming a people, a land, a nation, and a government. They are slowly moving from the period of judges and prophets, like the great Samuel, to the first of the kings: Saul and David.

Saul and David, once friends, are now enemies, bitter and violent and vindictive. Saul is king, but he sees David as a rival, a likely successor, and so he seeks to hunt him down and destroy him. David is a military genius as well as a psalmist and shepherd; he has the favor of God and the love of the people behind him. So Saul and David play a game of deadly hide and seek in the hills.

Finally David comes upon Saul and knows that God has delivered him into his hands. But David does not kill Saul.

Instead, he does him homage and tells Saul that the Lord will judge between them and will exact justice. David himself will take no action against Saul while he is king. At this, Saul is stricken with remorse.

Then the prophet Samuel dies, the man who had anointed Saul king and held Israel together prior to the kings. All Israel gathers to mourn and bury him. And now we meet Abigail, the wife of Nabal, who is wealthy and owns land in Carmel.

*Then David went down to the desert of Maon. There was a man of Maon who had property in Carmel; he was very wealthy, owning three thousand sheep and a thousand goats. At this time he was present for the shearing of his flock in Carmel. The man was named Nabal, his wife, Abigail. The woman was intelligent and attractive, but Nabal himself, a Calebite, was harsh and ungenerous in his behavior. When David heard in the desert that Nabal was shearing his flock, he sent ten young men, instructing them: "Go up to Carmel. Pay Nabal a visit and greet him in my name. Say to him, 'Peace be with you, my brother, and with your family, and with all who belong to you. I have just heard that shearers are with you. Now, when your shepherds were with us, we did them no injury, neither did they miss anything all the while they were in Carmel. Ask your servants and they will tell you so. Look kindly on these young men, since we come at a festival time. Please give your servants and your son David whatever you can manage.' "*

*When David's young men arrived, they delivered this message fully to Nabal in David's name, and then waited. But Nabal answered the servants of David: "Who is David? Who is the son of Jesse? Nowadays there are many servants who run away from their masters. Must I take my bread, my wine, my meat that I have slaughtered for my own shearers, and give them to men who come from I know not where?" So David's young men retraced their steps and on their return they reported to him all that had been said. Thereupon David said to his men, "Let everyone gird on his sword." And so everyone, David included, girded on his sword. About four*

*hundred men went up after David, while two hundred re-*
*mained with the baggage (1 Samuel 25:2-13).*

This is the backdrop for the story. We begin with a description of a man and woman, husband and wife. One is intelligent and attractive, and the other is harsh and ungenerous.
David needs provisions, has heard of Nabal, and sends his
men to prepare for his arrival with his army—those who have
been loyal to him during the time that Saul has been hunting
him. And it is a festival time. Nabal is not only rude and
unresponsive to David's request, but he breaks the code of
hospitality that is fundamental to the peoples of the desert.
He is required by law to give to those who beg from him.
This is true even if he had been a beggar, let alone a wealthy
man who just doesn't want to be bothered with someone he
doesn't know. It is a double breach of courtesy because it is a
time of festival, a religious and social occasion and a respite
from fighting. What Nabal does is equivalent to a slap in the
face, a provocation to battle. And that is what is going to
happen.

Saul, David, and Nabal are all violent men, trained in war
and intrigue with a code of their own, but brutal in the face
of opposition. It is a time in Israel's history when the people
are becoming a nation, developing a culture that is not
nomadic, and yet there are still courtesies they are expected
to honor. David follows the protocol and Nabal refuses him;
in fact, he insults him and baits him—hinting that he could
just be another runaway slave. David, accustomed to fighting
and to having people not only know who he is, but honor
him, is furious. He responds with violence.

War has been a constant reality since history has been
recorded. The Israelites may be worshipers of one God who
has no face, no form, but he is a warring god, defender of the
people. Further, God's servants and kings at that time are not
known for either justice or mercy. Israel is young in its understanding of religion, and it is fierce in its attempts to survive
in this promised land that is nonetheless alien and occupied.
A just and equal society is not even dreamed of.

There are internal conflicts and divisions in Israel as well.

It is a time of skirmishes, a time when differences are usually settled with bloodshed and displays of strength. God is inter-mingled in all of this—on this side or that, with this person or that person, depending on fidelity to the covenant and regard for the people. At this moment in the story God is on David's side, and one day David will become king. Already he is used to getting his own way, being obeyed, and not being ignored or insulted or refused. His reaction, harsh as it appears to us, is not unusual. After all, look at how we deal with shows of force by other countries today. Our world may be much more sophisticated, but it is just as brutal and violent, just as full of jealousy, greed, and personal reactions. But Abigail intervenes.

> *Nabal's wife Abigail was informed of this by one of her servants, who said: "David sent messengers from the desert to greet our master, but he flew at them screaming. Yet these men were very good to us. We were done no injury, neither did we miss anything all the while we were living among them during our stay in the open country. For us they were like a rampart night and day the whole time we were pasturing the sheep near them. Now, see what you can do, for you must realize that otherwise evil is in store for our master and for his whole family. He is so mean that no one can talk to him." Abigail quickly got together two hundred loaves, two skins of wine, five dressed sheep, five seahs of roasted grain, a hundred cakes of pressed raisins, and two hundred cakes of pressed figs, and loaded them on asses. She then said to her servants, "Go on ahead; I will follow you." But she did not tell her husband Nabal (1 Samuel 25:14-19).*

Abigail must be loved by her servants. In fact, it appears that they often go to her to offset what Nabal does. Her relationship with the servants, even the shepherds who tend the flock in the desert, is one of open communication and even shared feelings about events and people, including her husband, their master. The story is really set in motion by an unnamed servant who speaks to Abigail on behalf of all the other servants and the whole household. The servants know

that to refuse hospitality to those who have given you protection and safe passage in open country is stupid and rash
behavior. It can get them all killed or sold into slavery.

Abigail moves quickly. She is organized, efficient, and cool-
headed. She knows exactly what she has to do to stop the
ensuing battle and slaughter of her household. She must undo
the insult and go bearing gifts to placate David. Further, she
is wise enough to act without consulting with her husband.
She is independent, careful, obeyed by her own servants, and
resourceful. She is a good judge of human nature, of character, and circumstances, and it seems she is more—she is
nonviolent, a peacemaker. She herself heads out to meet
David face to face before the army can get to her house.

*As she came down through a mountain defile riding on an ass,
David and his men were also coming down from the opposite
direction. When she met them, David had just been saying:
"Indeed, it was in vain that I guarded all this man's possessions in the desert so that he missed nothing. He has repaid
good with evil. May God do thus and so to David, if by morning I leave a single male alive among all those who belong to
him." As soon as Abigail saw David, she dismounted quickly
from the ass and, falling prostrate on the ground before David,
did him homage. As she fell at his feet she said:*

*"My lord, let the blame be mine. Please let your handmaid
speak to you, and listen to the words of your handmaid. Let
not my lord pay attention to that worthless man Nabal, for he
is just like his name. Fool is his name and he acts the fool. I,
your handmaid, did not see the young men whom my lord
sent. Now, therefore, my lord, as the LORD lives, and as you
live, it is the LORD who has kept you from shedding blood and
from avenging yourself personally. May your enemies and
those who seek to harm my lord become as Nabal! Accept this
present, then, which your maidservant has brought for my
lord, and let it be given to the young men who follow my lord.
Please forgive the transgression of your handmaid, for the
LORD shall certainly establish a lasting dynasty for my lord,
because your lordship is fighting the battles of the LORD, and
there is no evil to be found in you your whole life long. If*

*anyone rises to pursue you and to seek your life, may the life
of my lord be bound in the bundle of the living in the care of
the* LORD *your God; but may he hurl out the lives of your
enemies as from the hollow of a sling. And when the* LORD
*carries out for my lord the promise of success he has made
concerning you, and appoints you as commander over Israel,
you shall not have this as a qualm or burden on your conscience, my lord, for having shed innocent blood or for having
avenged yourself personally. When the* LORD *confers this benefit on your lordship, remember your handmaid"* (1 Samuel
25:20-31).

Abigail could teach classes in the practice of nonviolence
and peacemaking to individuals and nations. She follows a
pattern and plan but also knows that she is taking a chance.
She hopes that David will hear her and be able to listen to
the truth—not just about the situation and the stupidity of
her husband's actions, which could cause trouble, but also
about David's own response of personal vengeance, not fitting in a king that Yahweh protects. She brings gifts and goes
to meet him in person and immediately humbles herself
before him, pleading to be heard. She refers to herself as David's handmaid—slave or servant who lives to obey his command. And she explains her husband's behavior candidly,
admitting that it was foolish. But then she also explains that
she was not aware of the rude reception David's men received
and that she is acting to right the situation, and she offers the
gifts to his men. Then she draws God into the conversation,
connecting what is happening to David's relationship with
God, carefully pointing out what God does and intends to do
for David. She, for her part, stands with God; she does not
want David's reputation or conscience smeared with innocent
blood.

Abigail prays for David, blesses him and his future dynasty,
and then assumes responsibility for the transgression and
breach of hospitality and justice. She is smooth and crafty and
ingenious, comparing David's enemies to God hurling them
out as one would a stone in a slingshot, whirled about and
flung wide and far away from him! She obviously knows sto-

ries of David and alludes to David's own moment of triumph and glory as a weak and innocent and unaware shepherd fighting the professional soldier Goliath. She tells David that one day he will be the commander of all of Israel and when he is, he should remember her words of truth and remember her as well. She praises, accepts blame, blesses, tells the truth, and reminds David of God's power and the inappropriateness of personal vengeance. God is not an avenging God, but a just one. David does not need to prove his strength or express his rage at being humbled or slighted by killing others not responsible for one man's discourtesy.

Abigail is banking on David's basic goodness and justice, and she is attempting to teach him the basics of mercy and nonviolence — even why he should do it — in imitation of God! And David, who has won the favor of God, responds:

> "Blessed be the LORD, the God of Israel, who sent you to meet me today. Blessed be your good judgment and blessed be you yourself, who this day have prevented me from shedding blood and avenging myself personally. Otherwise, as the LORD, the God of Israel, lives, who has restrained me from harming you, if you had not come so promptly to meet me, by dawn Nabal would not have had a single man or boy left alive." David then took from her what she had brought him and said to her: "Go up to your home in peace! See, I have granted your request as a personal favor" (1 Samuel 25:32-35).

David recognizes that she has seen the situation even more clearly than he has, and he acknowledges that God has sent her to stop him from shedding blood. Her quick response in going to meet him — an enemy — has turned him into a friend who now grants her a personal favor. She can go in peace, and so can her household, David himself and his men, and the land. Peace, shalom, wholeness, balance, and a bond between people — all have been repaired by her humility, graciousness, words, actions and willingness to put herself between David and Nabal.

The image of Abigail going to meet David seated on an ass evokes images of Palm Sunday and Jesus coming into the city of Jerusalem, David's city. It calls to our minds the prince of peace attempting to meet his enemies and intervene by putting his own body on the line as the blood price for peace. Abigail is a teacher of peace, a truth-teller. She is sent by God, and so she is a prophetess, changing history and interjecting into the bloody history of Israel a moment of peacemaking, of nonviolence, of a respite from fighting and from dealing with problems by escalating violence and bloodshed.

Abigail returns home to find her husband at a party and drunk, and so she waits until morning to tell him what she has done and how David has reacted to her words and gifts. The reaction of Nabal to his wife's story is remarkable: "At this his courage died within him, and he became like a stone" (1 Samuel 25:37). Ten days later, Nabal is struck by the Lord and dies.

David hears of Nabal's death and blesses God that he did not kill him, but that it was God who punished Nabal for his own evil deeds. God is the judge and the justice, not David. Thus David learns how to govern in God's name and not use his power for personal vendettas but rather to shepherd the people and fight only God's battles not his own. A remarkable lesson to learn, and from a woman!

Upon Nabal's death David immediately sends a proposal of marriage to Abigail. Abigail responds just as quickly and surely to this request as she did when she and her household, even her harsh and ungenerous husband, were in danger:

*"Your handmaid would become a slave to wash the feet of my lord's servants." She got up immediately, mounted an ass, and followed David's messengers, with her five maids following in attendance upon her. She became his wife, and David also married Ahinoam of Jezreel. Thus both of them were his wives; but Saul gave David's wife Michal, Saul's own daughter, to Palti, son of Laish, who was from Gallim (1 Samuel 25:41-43).*

The story ends with Abigail disappearing into a harem of other wives, willing and grateful even to wash David's servants' feet. This image of foot washing is important in both the Hebrew and Christian testaments. The gesture of washing another's feet was one of hospitality and service, but it was not required even of a wife to a husband or of a slave to a master because it was such an onerous task. Abigail humbles herself again, this woman who saves lives and acts as quickly as any general or tactician. She has been teacher, negotiator, reconciler, prophetess, and priestess, blessing David and calling on God to protect him and his dynasty. He returns the blessing and marries her.

Abigail is mentioned only twice more in the books of Samuel. She is taken captive by the Amelekites raiding near Ziklag but then rescued with another of David's wives, Ahinoam, who was married to David at the same time (1 Samuel 30:5, 18). And then, lastly, she bears David a son, Chileab, at Hebron and lives with David at Gath (2 Samuel 3:3). This is not much specific information, but enough to know that her life was not easy. The times she lived in were harsh, and the people she was a part of were violent. After all, even God describes them (and us) often as stubborn, hardhearted, and fickle. She knew war intimately, and she strove for peace. She knew insecurity, instability, violence, personal suffering, and a communal marriage. She was wife and mother. But to us she is a peacemaker in a world of war, one who practices active nonviolence and resistance to evil. She is a glimmer of hope in the midst of a bleak and harsh time.

Abigail offers glimpses of friendship, of personal intervention in historical events, lessening the bloodshed, if only in small ways. She is an alternative to hate, rage, and rash reactions. She is humble, meek, prayerful, and quick-witted. She is a wise woman, wiser by far than David, the one who will be king in Israel. But she does her part to offer another reality, even though it does not seem to have been much imitated — then or now. She knew, even then, that God is a God of life, not death, and is served by life and its protection, not by dealing in death. She approached David with confidence, a confidence born of reflection (she knew of him and his exploits and conflicts) and of hope in God, who is just. Her idea of God is more developed, more mature, and more in line with Jesus' God than David's. She uses gifts, words, and her person instead of force as her means to an end — a peaceful end where all benefit and none loses. Both can leave each other with dignity, having learned to trust and listen as well as situate a personal matter in the larger context of God's ways on earth.

Abigail is foremost a woman of justice and peace, an image of the kingdom to come with the presence of the Messiah. What she has learned in faithfulness, prayer, and reflection, she acts upon. Thus she brings God into a situation where God had been excluded and cast out. She knows, even in the midst of oppression and wars for liberation and struggles for power, that God is not served by war and death and the shedding of innocent blood or by avenging one's own petty experiences. She knows, in the gift of wisdom given to her, and shared in this event with David, that it is better to reconcile, to heed the truth of another, to go out and meet the other, and to humble oneself to attempt to forge a solution that blesses God in all the parties involved. She knows how to look for the goodness in David and call that forth. She knows what injustice is — both in her husband and in David. She can see clearly the effects of injustice and how widespread and long-term they will be if David acts foolishly, as her husband did. She is careful about providing concrete suggestions and alternatives to what is planned — gifts, food for his men, worship of God, trust, and a prayer for David's success, along with a mention of being remembered. She brings gifts of peace, but she herself is the gift and eventually, when the time presents itself, David is wise enough to take the offering and keep Abigail in his life.

Abigail's name means "my father's joy" or "joy of my father" — a daughter of faith, peace, and humility, a delight to her father's heart, much as Jesus will be a delight and joy to the Father. She knows something of Jesus' Father even in the harshness of war and the early experiences of Israel and God. Abigail has a consciousness that can form the conscience of David, an awareness of justice that David must come to understand time and again. She is his equal, though she describes herself as his servant and handmaid. There is no mention of fear in her, though she must have been afraid. But she is a woman of courage, of heart, who brings joy to many. For the product of peace and justice is joy!

Abigail could be the patron saint of all women who find themselves in violent situations because of the tendency of others to solve problems by violence. She could be the one remembered by many women today who seek justice and protection for women battered, raped, caught in war zones, and counted — for once — among those killed, maimed, or left as refugees and survivors. Abigail is the model for all those who negotiate and deal in conflict management and nonviolent action, for those who are ambassadors and trainers in nonviolent resistance to evil and structures. She is a good practical teacher of all men and women who go out to meet the enemy and try to make friends, who know what is going on in the world and act, sometimes putting themselves in humiliating positions or in jeopardy to stop others from being harmed and to seek an end to misunderstandings and petty quarrels.

Abigail is sister to all those caught in armed conflicts, low-intensity warfare, and national viciousness. She is a woman of her times calling out quietly and forcefully to men and women of our times that God is a God of justice and life and peace. She reminds us that justice lies primarily in the hands of God, not in the hands of those who have power, or armies, or even at times the legal right to extract justice. Justice comes in unknown and unexpected ways — not always as quickly as in Nabal's case, but it comes in God's time and in God's ways, not violently and not catching the innocent in its grasp.

Abigail teaches a lesson to a future king. This lesson must be learned anew in every generation, in every nation, and in every heart, whether powerful and strong, or weak and without earthly power, or else we will all perish. Abigail is a respite in the history of war, a lull in the fighting, but she also models an alternative that can be practiced, experienced, and incorporated into daily life as well as in national politics, business, schools, and parishes. She patterns behavior that is necessary and vital to the continued existence of humankind and the daily life of peace among all peoples.

Abigail is the heart of God reconciling in small ways, hoping those in the world will notice, learn, and take to heart the reality of a kingdom of justice and peace. She is joy to the heart of God and to all peoples of all times. She is a statement of peace and its possibility and that reminds us of an old Finnish proverb: "Joy is the daughter of peace." The earth needs Abigails, lots of them, young and old, male and female, of all nations. Abigail reveals another proverb from Mexican Americans: "La gracia no es vivir, la gracia es saber vivir" (The blessing is not in living, but in knowing how to live").

Our spirituality, prayers, and reflections must incorporate the quick-wittedness and courage on behalf of others that Abigail demonstrates. However she prayed, she learned ahead of others how to bring peace in time of war, how to effect change in those in power, and how to stop bloodshed. Any spirituality that does not lead to engagement in the making of peace, the crafting of nonviolent responses to contemporary events and relationships is not worthy of being called a spirituality. Nabal is selfish and rude, disregarding courtesy and hospitality. David is rash, selfish, and violent, thinking only of his own ego and pride. It is Abigail and the servants who see what the effects of such actions will be and move to stop the violence. Abigail works with others to demilitarize her small piece of the promised land and to offer solutions to enmity, even offering her life as ransom so that others might live.

"Blessed are the peace-makers they shall be called the children of God." In every generation, in every nation and land, men and women live as peacemakers, children of God, working for justice, organizing, and imitating Abigail, who imitates God. Or did God decide to follow Abigail's lead and take the ass into Jerusalem in memory of a woman approaching David generations earlier and trying to make peace?

# 9

## JERUSALEM

T here are two short pieces in the gospel of Luke that reveal Jesus lamenting over the city of Jerusalem and lamenting its people who have missed his coming because of their blindness, stubbornness, and hard-heartedness. Each is short, emotionally descriptive of Jesus' feelings and prayer, and both leave us with a terrible sense of aloneness, loss, and separateness. They speak of endings, of what might have been and will not be, and of deep abiding sorrow and utter loneliness. They are almost too human, too hard to bear. They reveal both sorrow and the prophecy of coming destruction. One is a lamentation in the tradition of Jeremiah and the mourning songs and poems of deep personal loss. The other is a short, direct address to the city and its inhabitants. Both appear in the text at crucial points toward the end of Jesus' public ministry and close to his impending betrayal and crucifixion. They reveal a Jesus who knows intimately the experience of rejection, hate, of being ignored and despised. They reveal Jesus as one of those not counted—like women, children, the poor, the oppressed. In fact, one of these texts describes Jesus as a mother bird, a hen wanting desperately to gather her chicks under her wing to protect and care for them.

The first segment is addressed to the city, and so to the nation, its leaders, and its people:

> "O Jerusalem, Jerusalem, you slay the prophets and stone those who are sent to you! How often have I wanted to gather your children together as a mother bird collects her young under her wings, and you refused me! Your temple will be abandoned. I say to you, you shall not see me until the time comes when you say, 'Blessed is he who comes in the name of the Lord' " (Luke 13:34-35).

Reactions to this passage are mixed, as are the metaphors in the text. Jesus sees himself as one who has been sent to the city, a prophet rejected and about to be slain. Yet there is the great tenderness and vulnerability in Jesus, who sees himself as a mother bird wanting to draw her defenseless young under her wing. The image of gathering, collecting his own about him, recalls a shepherd gathering sheep, or the church gathering for liturgy and worship. The reference to the temple that will be abandoned, as Jesus will be abandoned, adds another layer to the sorrow and utter sense of helplessness. Jesus is mixing both the warning and the starkness of the prophet's words with a plea for repentance and acceptance of the word of God, even now. Jesus' words are filled with allusions to the prophet Jeremiah, who was charged with the impossible task of bringing Jerusalem back to its senses before it was too late, and his failure to do so, followed by the destruction of the temple, the ruin of the city, and the exile of the people.

The burden of the prophets has always been the stubbornness of the people, and it has been a heavy burden. Their words are like fire, like a hammer shattering rocks (Jeremiah 23:29), and yet most times the rocks don't break. Rather, the people are like a wall against the words and warnings, and the prophet steadfastly continues preaching, unheard and rejected at best, sought out and more often than not killed.

The calls to mercy and tenderness are interspersed with dire warnings and sharp language that is pointed at the hearts of the leaders and the people as Jesus continues toward Jerusalem (Luke 19:28).

Jesus weeps over his own, his own city, his own people, his own nation, his own heritage, what had been his hope for those he was sent to, those given into his care. His visitation — that could have meant rejoicing, a new beginning, the long-awaited hope come to fulfillment — has come to nothing. He rides an ass, approaching the city from the descent of Mount Olivet, his disciples and a crowd crying out. But their exultation will be short lived. In a few days the crowd will be crying out for blood, for execution and death, forgetful of this short fleeting moment of acceptance. Jesus has much to weep about and yet he weeps for these people who are so unconscious, so blind, so violent, so unfaithful to God.

Jesus is both the prophet of Israel, the Word of the Lord come again to the people, and the Suffering Servant, the one who will untiringly seek to draw his people back to God at any cost. He is the mother bird that will give its life to the snare trying to save its young, giving them time to fly to safety on their weak wings. The image is old in the Jewish tradition, often in reference to an eagle's wings. This image is full of comfort and the promise of protection:

> I will raise you up on eagles' wings
> and bear you on the breath of dawn;
> I will make you to shine like the sun
> and I will hold you in the palm of my hand.

Eagles mate forever, faithful until death. They build their nests high on cliffs and rocks away from any predators. When the young are born, usually no more than three, they are large, ungainly and awkward, unable to fly, helpless and in need of constant protection, watchfulness, and feeding. The eagles hunt for food and chew it up and put it into the mouths of the young eagles hourly until they are strong enough to fly. When they are ready to be taught how to fly, the eagles dump the nest over, sending the young ones out into the air. They flap wildly, in a panic, and then almost get the hang of it, but they are weak, unused to flying, and they begin to fall. Then one of the adult eagles swoops down and comes up under the young one that is falling and lifts it on its own wings, higher and higher, giving it a needed rest—and then pulls up abruptly again. And the young one goes at it again, until it tires. Again and again the mother and father birds lift their young on their own wings and carry them until they have learned the strength that is dormant in their own smaller wings. It takes about fifteen minutes, and then all three of the young can fly and not one has come anywhere near the ground.

Is this the image of the mother bird that Jesus has in mind: the mighty and proud soaring eagle? Or is he thinking of an ordinary hen, a weak and vulnerable bird that can also be fierce in its protection of its young, fighting and pecking at its enemies, moving quickly to gather its own in clucking gestures and outspread wings? Either image fits Jesus, for he will both gather his own for the eucharist in this last week of his life and they will later be scattered and run in fear. Jesus will be destroyed, hung outside the city, crucified on the city's garbage heap, the constant abode of carrion birds. But he will also know the glory of the eagle on the wings of the Spirit in the rising morning sun of resurrection and new life. Jesus' tears are of sorrow and lamentation, human tears of rejection and sheer frustration — he has given his all, his best, the word and the presence of the Lord, the image of his Father, merciful, just, tenderhearted and seeking only the life of the sinner. Now he will give his last word, his blood, his body, his life in this last attempt to get the people to listen to him.

As Jesus begins the last portion of his way of the cross, there are a few who watch and respond with weeping and mourning.

> *A great crowd of people followed him, including women who beat their breasts and lamented over him. Jesus turned to them and said: "Daughters of Jerusalem, do not weep for me. Weep for yourselves and for your children. The days are coming when they will say, 'Happy are the sterile, the wombs that never bore and the breasts that never nursed.' Then they will begin saying to the mountains, 'Fall on us,' and to the hills, 'Cover us.' If they do these things in the green wood, what will happen in the dry?" (Luke 23:27-31).*

The women weep for Jesus, and yet Jesus turns their tears away from him, back toward themselves and their children, toward those who are to come after them. It is here that Jesus points out to us that the way of the cross is not just his, but ours and others. The women express compassion and remorse in groans, beating their breasts in sadness, sorrow, and mourning; it is a time for feeling for and feeling with others, with Jesus. There is a shared horror at what we do to each other in violence, in fear, in rejection, in sin. There is a communion in suffering that is not connected to friendship, or even knowing the person, but recognizing another in their

deepest place of vulnerability — as another human being. But
Jesus' words deflect their pity away from himself and his sufferings and humiliation. It seems there is something worse in
the world than this kind of innocent and unnecessary suffering. Worse are those who do injustice to others, those without
pity or compassion, those who are responsible in their actions
and deeds for stopping life and inflicting pain and horror on
others, those who practice evil while claiming to believe in
God, those who sin. What eventually will come upon them,
in the fullness of God's time and judgment, will be worse than
this suffering of the innocent, this crucifixion of the Word of
justice, mercy, and hope. Even in the midst of his pain Jesus
reminds the women and us of what is most horrible and pit-
iable — human beings who are not human, not obedient to the
heart of what it means to live, that is, to give life and sustain
that life and share it with others.

Tears of compassion must also be tears of penance, of the
wrenching that comes with change, of crying out against
insensitivity, self-interest, lack of concern, of collusion with
evil institutions and structures and personal abuses against
others. The spiral of violence must be arrested by compassion
that becomes admonition, penance publicly atoning for and
with the victims. The tears must become the lamentation of
the prophets, with Jesus weeping over Jerusalem, because a
city, a nation, a whole people missed his meaning, his presence and power, and the possibility for change, for hope for
others. It is Jesus' lamentation over the church, over us. We
must look to and know who inflicts death, deals with death
and destruction and profits by it. We must acknowledge how
to participate in it and weep for our own complicity and what
we do that causes others to suffer needlessly.

We have to go to the heart of what causes misery and
injustice here and now. Too often we adapt to things as they
are, only weeping and being touched when injustice gets
close to us personally. We cannot just weep over situations.
We have to learn how to intervene. We have to learn not just
to stand there, like the majority of the people in the crowd.
It is the moment for conversion. Compassion is a dead end if
it does not lead us to life, to move, to denounce prophetically

why this misery exists, why the human condition has gotten this far out of line, why there is this terrible destruction of human life and dignity. And if we don't, it will affect us eventually and our children.

This moment on the way of the cross has Jesus confronting us and saying: Do not concentrate on my pain. Look to what is around you and the effects of individual choices on the pain of the world, because it is going to affect all of us whether we acknowledge it or not. Jesus is still warning us, pleading for change, for penance, for a stop to what we do and allow to happen in our midst. He is still the Suffering Servant concerned about others. He is still the mother bird trying to save her children and her children's children. Even in his own pain Jesus the innocent child looks to the other children in the family and tells the truth. Even in his own death march Jesus' spirit is remembering Jerusalem and the children of God and all the suffering caused by injustice, violence, and the worship of powers other than the God of justice and love. Even now, Jesus has the words of the prophet Hosea (10:8) on his lips and yet Jesus is probably also feeling the deeper love that Hosea was always describing:

> *When Israel was a child I loved him,*
> *out of Egypt I called my son.*
> *The more I called them,*
> *the farther they went from me,*
> *Sacrificing to the Baals*
> *and burning incense to idols.*
> *Yet it was I who taught Ephraim to walk,*
> *who took them in my arms;*
> *I drew them with human cords,*
> *with bands of love;*
> *I fostered them like one*
> *who raises an infant to his cheeks;*
> *Yet, though I stooped to feed my child,*
> *they did not know that I was their healer.*
> *(Hosea 11:1-4)*

Jesus is still the mother, the healer, the father who seeks to touch the child, to draw his children closer with loving kindness, tenderhearted glances, and affection, and is re-buffed.

Jesus will be as faithful to his friends and enemies as he is to his own Father-God. He will hang on for dear life for a dearer life, he will be the faithful child of God, the beloved child, the servant whose tears will be turned into cascading tears of joy, of shining tears on the face of one risen from the tomb, of radiant tears like the first rays of the sun, of the Sun of Justice, the Son of Man bringing tears of hope once again to his friends when they are still locked in rooms of fear and despair. There is a time for tears, a time for faithfulness, a time for endurance, and a time for exaltation. There is a time for truth and a time for justice — all times.

In Latin America there is a saying: the other side of faith-fulness is endurance. Many endure because so many others are unfaithful. These moments of weeping and lamenting on the way to the cross are associated most often with women, because women cry more often in our culture. But these are tears that reveal humanness, compassion, and God's desire for us to embrace one another as the presence of God. Those whose hearts belong to God, who serve others and have learned to trust the mother bird, the father eagle, the child Jesus, and the winged Spirit.

It will be the women who go to the tomb to anoint the dead body of one they love. This is a corporal act of mercy that they know will be hard; hard grief, hard remembering, but also hard because they know there is a stone that blocks the entrance to the tomb. But perhaps it was tears that rolled the stone away, the tears of all those who have suffered unjustly and have borne in their bodies the reality of violence and injustice as their share of the sufferings of the cross of Christ. Perhaps it was the tears that began in compassion and solidarity and became the cries of the prophets in opposition to powers and authorities and structures that serve only the powerful. Perhaps it was the tears of Jesus, the tears of the Spirit, and the tears of Jesus' God that loosened the stone and opened the tomb to hope. Jesus, the child, the woman, the man of truth and justice resists containment in tombs and burial chambers and prefers instead to walk among us and dry the tears from our eyes or turn them into joy. The Living One does not dwell and cannot be found among the bones and in the places that resist love.

Jesus, the crucified one, is the image of the One not counted, forgotten, cast aside, rejected. Yet this Jesus is the One God raised from the dead. Now this Jesus remembers all those not counted and puts them at the head of the parade. And all women and children and men, all humankind and earth and its creatures sing for the "great things this God has done for them." This is the way God's stories go. This is the Word of the Lord.

# Afterword

This book is not just *my* thoughts, insights, and work. It has been written by the church "of the uncounted" scattered in many out-of-the-way places, among people seeking to make the Word into flesh in today's world. These people constantly remind me that originally the scriptures were lived, breathed, and told in community, and only later put down on paper. But for them to have power and meaning today, these words on paper need to be taken off the page and put back into the mouths of believers and then lived in flesh and blood, individually and collectively.

There are a number of assumptions that I have made that need to be stated so that the reader will understand some of the history and power of where and how these words were conceived and born. They are not mine, but belong to many. All I have done is to try to gather them together in some sort of framework and extend them into the larger tradition of the church universal. They were born in a church of hope, a church of disciples and justice, suffering, and peace. These assumptions can be kept in mind as you use this book, by yourself or with others, in study and prayerful reflection on the scriptures.

First, *the text of the scriptures is inspired*. That means simply that for every generation, every group, every language, every people, the text hides the mystery of salvation, of conversion, and of the kingdom in its words, structure, and meaning. It is like ground that needs to be dug into, overturned and seeded, watered, and tended with continual care. It is full of potency, of hidden mines of the Spirit, of insight and understanding for all those who approach it with reverence.

Not only is the text inspired, the context is also inspired.

Although context traditionally refers to the portions of text that immediately precede and follow the portion being studied, I am not primarily referring to that. For myself and others, the context is the group of people reading, listening, and being exposed to the text. It includes the people's backgrounds, struggles, sin, gifts, world situations, and personal lives. Every group that gathers in the context of the Spirit to pray and to listen to the word of the Lord finds itself in the midst of the Lord. The presence of God suffuses the text and lets it enter the people's ears, minds, hearts, and souls.

Second, *the scriptures are written for conversion.* The intent of the scriptures is not so much to inform as to convert. This conversion is directed toward the individual first of all, but the individual in community, in church, and then to the community and the church. Conversion is about change, about altering our mind-set, behavior patterns, beliefs, and relationships with others and the world. It is about the struggle between good and evil. It is about discipleship, about sin and virtue, about the practice of community and worship. It encompasses prayer, ethics, morality, economics, politics, sociology—all of existence. Conversion seeks to make life whole, holy and pleasing to God as sacrifice, as offering, as incentive for others, as encouragement. It happens on the levels of understanding and knowledge and insight; in the area of action, decision-making and establishing priorities; and in the realm of prayer, emotions, worship, and the sense of being bound to God, to others, and to all creation. To hear the word of God is to change. If we do not change, we have not heard. Indeed, to hear the word of God is to be censored, to be judged, to be challenged, to be altered, even radically reformed. And so to hear the word of God on a continual basis within the context of a believing community means to be radically changed as a group, as a people, as a community; it also means to be comforted and encouraged as part of that people of the word.

The scriptures call us to recommit our lives to following Jesus and the community of believers, to rededicate ourselves to bringing the kingdom of God to earth in our history. This approach to the scriptures can be revolutionary. The scrip-

tures use us to do the work of God. They reveal the depth of
what it means to be a follower of Jesus and they confront us
with a mirror, a reflection of what our lives are supposed to
be. They can bring us up short, make us gasp for breath, and
make us see the truth about our belief or lack of it, our life in
conformity with our belief, or the inconsistencies of how we
live out our belief in public. In this kind of reading of the
scriptures we are all sinners, all the time. To sin means "to
miss the mark" — the mark of our baptism, the mark that seals
us and claims us for God in Christ. But it is as sinners that
the Good News comes to us and God saves us and becomes
part of our lives and hearts and homes. Experiencing scripture
as conversion follows a process in which scripture:

— confronts us with the truth and convicts us of sin;

— challenges us to change and reveals what we need to
change in our lives, individually and as a community;

— comforts us in our struggle to make the word of the Lord
come true in our lives.

Third, *the scriptures should never be used to prove anything.*
The scriptures, especially the four gospels, are faith statements
of already-believing communities. Those who wrote the gospels were set on reminding their communities of baptized
Christians of what could be the depth and meaning of their
lives as disciples of Jesus, children of the Father, and people
of the Spirit. The gospels were intended for ordinary believers
and people who found themselves in historical situations of
persecution, of moral choices and dilemmas, and of relationships that severely tried their faith, people who found themselves stumbling in their convictions and sinning in their lives.
The communities of Matthew, Mark, Luke, and John, like the
early Israelites, were having difficulty living up to their bap-
tismal promises, covenant agreements, and community obli-
gations in the midst of a world that pressured them to
conform and persecuted them, sometimes incredibly harshly.
These communities were trying to rely on the Spirit given to
the church to help them transform their lives to bring the
kingdom in history, and to make disciples in the whole world
as Jesus had commissioned them.

All the gospels were written after the shattering experience

of the cross and the confusing yet death-destroying experience of the resurrection that gave birth to the early church
and the first Christian communities. All the gospels seek in
some way to mine that one experience: the Father raising
Jesus from the dead, shattering the hold of death on the
human race and testifying to the validity of the Son's words
and life as revealing God's presence among the people
through the power of the spirit of truth and justice. It is the
resurrection that provoked and evoked not only the faith of
the church, the hope of the community, and the love that was
apparent among them, but also the need to remember and to
enact and live out that faith, hope, and love daily in their
communities as witnesses to the world of the power of God
in history.

The reflections in this book were done in the context of
storytelling, story reading, and proclaiming that are unfinished. The story really begins when the reading and the discussion are over and the people begin to practice what they
have heard. These stories of the scriptures are our common
heritage and base as Christians and believers in Jesus' story
of God and the kingdom and what it means to be human and
full of grace, having found favor in the eyes of God. These
reflections were written as commentary on the text, as filler
in the spaces between the words. They are midrash, stories
around the story, stories within and under and laced through
the story. They are true, and evocative of the truth that is
oftentimes submerged in other things in our lives. They seek
to mine the depths of the Spirit's presence, by grace, in the
word, in the community, and in the future. They are true
because they judge us and the world about justice, about sin,
and about evil. They are true because they tell us who we are
by the life, death, and resurrection of Jesus, who we are in
the universal church of all those who have gone before us in
faith and together with us still wait for the fullness of the
kingdom and redemption to come to the earth. They are true
because they call us home, call us to holiness, call us to
accountability in community, and call us to stand in the presence of God and be seen, both individually and together, for
what we are and what we are not yet. They are true because

they are stories of becoming, unfinished and waiting for us to grasp hold of them—or better yet, to be grasped hold of by the Spirit in communities and made more in the image and likeness of God.

God is trinity—community, dialogue, a conversation of love, a presence of hope and possibility, redeeming grace, mercy and justice balanced together, harmony and all that leans toward gracefulness, especially in the face of evil, unnecessary suffering and sin and destruction. God is Jesus, son of Mary, son of Joseph, son of David and Jewish, son of God, son of Man, Lamb of God, son of justice, sun, and all the endearments of the Jewish people and the prophets who long awaited his coming. God is a child, a poor one, an outcast, unexpected, heralded but not understood, not exactly what anybody had or has in mind and more than anything anyone could expect or hope for—and more and more and more so that we are always called to believe, to risk, to go beyond words, images, and standard understandings. But, first and foremost, God is communal, three, and so has room for four and more and more—the whole world within the embrace of the Trinity.

A note about interpretations of the text. Common sense rules. Remember to look at what comes before and after a story. After all, each story has a beginning and continues to an end. Keep that end in mind—cross and resurrection—because all the stories were written after that fact and in light of that reality. Think about whose story you are reading and the overall intent and direction of that particular story. Don't mix and match the stories or compare them to other stories, unless it helps clarify something that gives you insight or calls you to conversion. And don't take lines, phrases, or images out of context and make them mean something that common sense says contradicts the meaning of the overall message of the gospel.

Communal interpretations of the text are the norm, rather than the perceptions of an individual. The stories are about us, all of us, from the beginning of time. They are not just about those folk back then, but us now, too. And community isn't just the group we're in at the moment, the parish or church we belong to—it's more, always more. It includes believers world-wide, the universal church in other countries and continents. It's all those who have gone before us in faith and struggled to put into practice their understanding of the text, those who have lived on the hopes and beliefs that the stories brought forth in them. It is the living, now, who struggle against terrible odds to make the stories come true in the midst of persecution and hardship, to keep the hopes alive, and to offer alternatives to those in darkness and death's long shadow. Sometimes this living of the word is referred to or known as the tradition of the church—the teaching of the institution, the magisterium, but it is the belief and life-line of the people of God, the church at its heart. And so, communal interpretation is always the norm.

There are two special groups that must be taken into consideration whenever there is any doubt or question of meaning. The first group is the poor, for the Good News is written with them in mind, for them and for their heartening. Jesus says this often. The "poor" means literally the poor according to the dictionary: those in jeopardy of life, those lacking the basic necessities for human living—food, clothing, shelter, education, medicine and health care, jobs, human dignity, and hope for the future. They live without security, without much possibility of change or hope for themselves and their children. They are the masses of people in the world in our country and others. They are the ones in any group, society, or institution not counted by the dominant ones. They are not heavily invested in the existing structures and groups and so do not have a great deal to protect or defend. They are not the ones who ordinarily benefit from change. They are often simply ignored, not noticed, not counted, and so they are poor. But they are the beloved of God, the ones first noticed, heard, and remembered by the poor one of God who became human and dwelled among us.

The second group is just as crucial to remember and include in any discussion of a particular text: they are those people who give witness and are martyred for their beliefs, their interpretations. Their giving of their lives is literally their last word on the matter, and those last words cannot be taken

lightly. So, for instance, any belief or interpretation of the
scriptures that any of the delegates of the word in Latin America or those who serve in missionary lands or more famous
witnesses like Oscar Romero spoke and staked their lives on
must become part of our interpretations of scripture.

What if you disagree with the community's belief and interpretation? There are three options. First, consider seriously
the possibility that you might be wrong. Second, you might
be partially right, but you may be so heavily invested in the
outcome that you can't see the other interpretations and clues
in the text because of culture, bias, race, or privilege. Whenever we are the ones who would immediately benefit from a
change in an interpretation, we must be careful and suspi-
cious of our own involvement and blindness in reading the
text to make it say what we want to it to say. And, third, you
might be right. This means being prophetic, and usually the
community may not endorse or put into practice your interpretation until you're dead, or at least until you have suffered
long and untiringly in the community for your own beliefs.
If you chose to stick to your own personal interpretation, then
you also have to accept a certain amount of persecution and
isolation that comes with separating yourself from the community's mainstream of belief. Above all, you must practice
consistently what that interpretation calls you to in society
and personal and public choices.

This prophetic understanding and underpinning of the stories is very important to keep in mind. The stories have to be
connected to the real poor, real suffering and death, real challenges to the establishment in society and church, and real
issues in justice, peace, poverty, and politics for the stories to
be of use in changing not just us but the world. Jesus is the
prophet of God, and so he is always speaking in the long
tradition and shadow of the prophets and poets who were
sent to the people whenever they disassociated themselves
from justice and from their neighbors and tried to practice
religion devoid of sacrifice and judgment.

The stories are not to be used on anybody else, but ourselves and our own group of believers. The scriptures are a
double-edged sword, but only for our hearts and minds and

lives; they are not to be taken up and used on others. They are hammers used to shatter rocks—but the rocks are us, not somebody else who suddenly springs to mind. The scriptures are sweet to the taste and good to chew on, but they usually go better in small doses, lingered over in community.

A good image of the scriptures is the Greek dessert pastry baklava. It is rich, about an inch thick and cut into inch squares. It is made of thin layers of philo dough, honey, nuts and butter pressed down and packed firmly together. A good pastry maker packs the dough into one hundred and twenty or more layers. And when we read the scriptures, we take one layer at a time and savor it. Each time we eat a layer and incorporate it into our flesh and blood, we can discover another layer and eat more. But not to swallow, digest, and incorporate it into our bodies and lives means that we may just keep eating the same layer over and over again. Whenever the word is incarnated in people, another layer of the word is revealed and presented to us to eat and feed on and take strength from, together. It is a many-course meal if we know how to eat it. Contained with the layers—the story—is the truth about us and the remedy for undoing what we have become and for making something new of our lives and communities, restoring, restructuring, and redeeming the times. Because of this process of seeing, unbecoming, and becoming whole again, we have to stay with the scriptural stories long enough for them to be seen as Good News, as hope for the future, as the reality of what we are by grace and the favor of God in Jesus Christ together.

Whenever there is doubt about the best interpretation (and there is always more than one true interpretation of scripture), the one that is most true is the one that calls us to the most radical change and conversion, alone or with others. The tradition of spirituality and ministry in the church has always been that gifts given to an individual are given for the community's benefit and growth, not for the individual's personal use and power. This works here as well. Our insights, interpretations, understandings of the scriptures and stories are not given for ourselves primarily but for the community. When we share our interpretation with others, we empty out a place inside ourselves and make room for the word of another, in the power of the Spirit, to enter and call us to conversion and hope. We are intimately bound to one another in the Spirit and the word. We must depend on others' interpretations of the text and their insights into our lives and weaknesses and strengths, because God speaks more clearly in another's voice and spirit than in our own. Incarnation says all of what we really know of God we learn from others, and they in turn learn from us. Whatever draws us back to Christ and community speaks the truest and is the best gift of the Spirit, even if it doesn't come across in the way expected or intended or particularly wanted or welcomed.

In our culture there is often a tendency to spiritualize, or personalize, or theologize on the text rather than to look at it hard and realistically. We are subtly and consistently affected by a too fundamentalist understanding of scriptures. We must work to steer clear of the individual or individuating nature of much of Western cultures and society. We say that Jesus died on the cross for our sins. That is a theological statement based upon past reality and the experience of a believing community after the fact of Jesus' death and resurrection. But to keep repeating that statement can rob the story and person of Jesus' life and death of any power to transform us, convict us, or grace us with the Spirit's meaning for our own lives. Jesus often tells his disciples they must deny themselves, pick up their cross, and follow in his footsteps.

When Jesus spoke of the cross, the images he evoked had nothing whatsoever to do with the theological notion of dying for sin. They were images of execution: long, tortuous, painful, public, and humiliating. Crucifixion was a form of capital punishment, legal — though unjust — that the Romans, the oppressor, the powerful used on the helpless, the poor and the oppressed, slaves, revolutionaries, anyone who spoke out against injustice. To say that Jesus died on the cross for our sins is often to ignore or forget that he died because he was dangerous to a society that wanted to hold unto its power. Jesus died on the cross for his beliefs, his idea of God, his preaching, his siding with the poor and the outcast. He died on the cross because he told the truth to power, putting himself in jeopardy for others, so that they might know life and the hope of freedom. His command to be ready to experience crucifixion as part of discipleship says that this is not just an historical account of one innocent man dying or a theological statement about why he died; it is a present-day reality that his disciples — all of us — must accept and deal with consistently.

The crucifixion and the cross are present in our world. Whenever the innocent die, whenever those who speak the truth are tortured, whenever those who work for justice are disappeared, whenever people die unnecessarily to sustain an unjust system or a government, whenever people die violently while others watch or participate — this is the cross. We are to pick up our cross, our place and reality of injustice, of brutality, of the suffering and the innocent, and follow Jesus.

We must rethink and reevaluate our theological and spiritual sayings to see the historical and concrete reality behind them. The gospel must be a living, breathing, present reality that moves us passionately to follow Jesus as Lord today in our world and to uncover the kingdom hidden in the midst of suffering and death. The cross is the way to salvation, the way home, the way the kingdom comes, the place God enters most powerfully in our lives. The cross is not a splinter but a huge piece of wood that all of us embrace at baptism as the sign and hope of life, of contradiction, of power and passion in the world where we follow in the footsteps of the broken and bent one, the child of God destroyed and still destroyed today. The cross is written into every line of every story. It is the ultimate wild card of the Spirit.

The scriptures are all about unity, community, balance, harmony, peace, and wholeness. All interpretations must push toward reconciliation, forgiveness, restoration, justice, and mercy in their decisions and relations and actions. They must be interpreted so that we are told to bend, to submit, to learn discipline, to obey, to let go of our ways of doing things, to compromise, and to know when something is important and crucial to stick to and when just to let go and let ourselves be reformed and refashioned.

If you wish to use the community method that brought

forth these reflections, keep in mind these suggestions and use the following questions after reading each portion of scripture.

1. What does the scripture make you feel?

2. Who is in the text? Where? When? What is happening?

3. Is there anything in the passage that makes you nervous, bothers, or upsets you? (This is a conversion question. Keep in mind that conversion usually starts at the edge of our awareness and acceptance and that change usually makes us uneasy.)

4. What are you going to do as an individual to make this passage come true in your present life? (Be specific and ask your community for insight.)

5. By baptism and confirmation we are all called to be prophets. Trying to use prophetic language, what is this passage saying about justice, peace, and the poor?

6. What are we, as a community, going to do to make this passage come true now in our lives, parish, and community? (Start simply, be specific and act. One response is to practice together works of mercy; the practice of hands-on-justice often leads to more work for justice.)

7. What in the passage gives you hope and joy?

Once upon a time God was lonely and, the Jewish teachers say, God created the earth and all that lives and breathes and dwells upon it, lastly us humans, because God needed and wanted someone to tell stories to—so they could come true. When our interpretations of scripture always lean toward justice, care for the poor, and the honor of God, the stories do come true. They reconcile us and draw us back to the basic unity that was given to us in the cross and resurrection of Jesus.